Chronicles of a Nomad: Book III

Thank you all for the love and support. I hope you are enjoying the ride of Chronicles of a Nomad

Chapter 1
Coffee House

I come in many shapes and sizes.
My silhouette can be breathtaking to the
natural eye of someone who has an
affinity for lavish things.
I embody the epitome of modern
marvels.
My many faces could indeed kindle
many appalling conclusions to the point
of a new beginning.
My hands give off mistaken reasoning,
awkward at sight but always pointing
in the right direction.
Who am I?
I am the preferred vision of beauty.

I feel what you feel.
I hurt when you hurt.
My hands are here to smooth, never to
disappoint.
My brain is not programmed for
failure but to embrace the will of right.

*I am affable, dependable; I come to be
known as what one counts on.*

*My essence is worldwide, global because
I am not environmentally challenged.
Though I may be small, my sound can
be heard from afar.
The distinction of my cacophony voice
streaks' the mood, sending a vast gravity
through the air!
Who am I?
I am the light that suppresses much of
the dark.*

*So who am I?
I am energy by day and night. I am
always in the mood for the most
unexpected presence.
I measure up to nothing else in this
world, a class A all on my own.
I run to the end never stopping in
between.
I give hope but also I give sorrow!
I am the ultimate thief lurking around
as you sleep stealing away the most
precious gift.
Who am I?
I am what one takes for granted, but
I'm what one can't live without.*

My life has changed tremendously since leaving Carolina. I have been living in Atlanta for three years now with Corey, Yanza, and Keith. The three of them are in college and I have been working as a writer for one of the local magazines. On my off days, my down time is usually spent in my poetry book. I took a liking to writing because it became an escape for me. I was never the schoolgirl so college for me was not an option but keeping our little family, the four of us created, together was one of the reasons I decided to move to Atlanta with the others.

It was about 4:15 in the afternoon. I was lying on my bed relaxing reading a poem that I had just finished while thinking I'd outdone myself because it surpassed my other writings. My writings are usually confusing to some because people tend to feed too much into it. Reading this one, you may think that I'm talking about a conceited person but in actuality it's about a clock. What I do is, I find something in my room or outside, focus on it, and let the words flow.

It was almost time for Keith to be getting out of class. I began to get myself together, going into the bathroom to shower and brush my teeth so I could be ready when he got here.

I was out of the shower and dressed by 5:30, but there was no sign of Keith. I called his phone repeatedly but there was answer. Yanza walked in and I asked her if she heard or seen either Keith or Corey.

She told me Corey was going over to Keith's track practice.

"They should be out at 6:30," she said.

"Why couldn't he let me know that they had practice? We had plans this afternoon," I said to her.

All she could say is that she was sorry and came in to hug me. I received the hug but it didn't cover up the hurt I felt.

"I thought you guys were getting better at communicating," she asked.

"I thought we were too."

I walked back in my room to grab my poetry book then I walked out the house.

The night swept over the sky. The breeze was soothing, a good night for a walk. As I walked thought about my relationship, and what I was doing there. Keith and I have been going through relationship issues for two years now, and every time I think things are getting better he does something like he did today.

I found myself walking through the park toward the bridge, one of my favorite areas, and saw the ducks and turtles swimming beneath. This spot has become my life. It's a relief not having to look over my shoulder and wonder if the police will be breaking down the door at any moment. Keith helped me escape that pain just to put me back into feeling something worse. The sound of night is calling out to me.

Close your eyes

Listen
Can't you hear it?
It's so peaceful, so serene
So different from anything you
ever heard
It's so close but yet so far
It's beautiful, relaxing
Just listen
Can't you feel the way it makes
your body move?
It's natural
It's is nature
It's you, it's me
Just listen

The words were just leaping onto the page out of my pen. It always amazes me how I can close my eyes and reopen them to a page filled with words that mean something to me.

Looking at the time I started back to my apartment. Suddenly my phone started to ring, it was Keith. I didn't hesitate, I just answered it.

"Hello," I said sternly.

"Hey, where are you. I'm at your crib," he said back to me.

"I'm out just taking in the night air," I replied.

"Are you coming back now, I want to see you," he asked. "

I will be there in a few," I said.

"Do you want me to wait," he asked.

"You seem to do what you want so it's up to you!" I said irritably before hanging up the phone. I had no other words for him. The night had turned peaceful and I wanted it to stay that way.

When I arrived back at my apartment, I found Yanza and Corey on the couch cuddled up. They have been through a lot as well, but they seemed to get through it every time. Keith needs to take a few lessons from his friend I thought.

I spoke to them both and continued to walk into my room so I wouldn't disturb them any further. When I got in there, to my surprise Keith was witting on my bed waiting for me. I didn't say a word to him, I grabbed some things and went into the bathroom to make myself more comfortable for the night.

Emerging from the bathroom dressed for bed, I walked all around, still not saying a word. Keith spoke up saying

"So you don't see me here?"

"I see you, but it's you that doesn't see me. I don't exist to you," I said back to him with anger in my voice.

"What are you talking about?"

"I'm talking about you not letting me know you had practice today. We had plans remember,"

"It was a last-minute call time, I'm sorry," he said while trying to sound sincere.

"I'm pretty sure your phone works just as well

as mine does," I said before continuing "You know what, I don't have time for this; I have work in the morning. You can let yourself out."

"But baby, I was looking forward to laying by you tonight. I'm sorry about today," he said.

"I'm getting tired of your apologies, they don't hold weight anymore; I suggest you leave now so you can catch the last bus or train home because Corey doesn't look like he's leaving anytime soon," I said as I was turning my TV off and getting into bed.

"Tina!"

"Good night," I responded.

I didn't look at him, but I heard when the door closed. I sighed and drifted off to sleep.

Chapter 2
Coffee House

"Ms. Mills," someone at my job is calling out.

"I'm right here Mr. Kobe," I said running into his office.

"Close the door and have a seat," he said.

I became a little nervous, but I did as I was told. He was staring at me as he was shifting his pen through his fingers. I remained silent because I didn't know what to expect. Sweat began to collect on my forehead from the nervousness and I prayed I wasn't fired. How am I going to pay my half of the rent, I thought to myself? Living in midtown is not cheap.

"You've been working for the company for a while now," he said. I just nod my head agreeing with his statement.

"Your articles have always added a little flavor to the magazine. Your poetic style of writing is captivating, and they've caught the eye of some very important people."

Partially relieved I started to smile a little but still was wondering what this means.

"I want to try you out as a field agent, something that can get you to stretch your legs a bit. At the H Lounge tonight there's a fashion show happening that I want you to cover. It will be different from phone interviews and answering email. I'm going to partner you up with Journey Rivers, he has experience as a field agent so you can learn from him. Ms. Mills, if you do this right it can become permanent and a promotion with better pay."

On the inside I am jumping for joy but remain calm on the outside.

"Thank you Mr. Kobe, thank you so much," I exclaimed.

Suddenly there came a knock on the door.

"Come in," said Mr. Kobe

"You wanted to see me," asked someone I've seen around the office but never officially met.

"Yes, I want you to meet La'Tina Mills. You're going to be working with her on the H Lounge Fashion Show tonight."

"Ms. Mills, this is Journey Rivers."

We shook hands and greeted one another.

"See my assistant for the information."

I told him thank you again and headed out with Journey. I was still trying to maintain my composure but the excitement was slowly coming out.

"You know you can go to the ladies room and let all that excitement out," Journey whispered to me as he was walking away.

I was a bit embarrassed and thought about it for a second but decided against it. Instead I walked over to Sharon, Mr. Kobe's assistant, and picked up the information for the show tonight. I looked it over and it had the address and start time of 7pm.

It's the end of the day and I'm packing up my things to head out for the night when Journey walks up.

"Are you ready for tonight?"

"Yeah," I responded.

"Did you do what he recommended and went in the restroom and screamed it out," he said, acting out the facial expression. He was a clown and it made me laugh, but I told him no.

"I should've, it was what I did when I became a field agent."

I couldn't help but to laugh at that because I can imagine him actually doing it.

"You have a beautiful smile," he said.

"Okay and this is my cue to make my exit," I responded as I got up to leave.

"Hey Hey, I'm sorry if I overstepped," he said.

"It's okay, but looking at the time I need to make a move if I'm going to make it on time tonight.

" Meet me there tonight at the front entrance at 6:30. Don't be late," he said as he walked away.

I made my way out the building and called Keith to tell him my good news, but his phone just rang with no answer. I hung up and redialed. This time, on the last ring he answered so I questioned him as to what he was doing. He said he was not near his phone at that time. I felt a bit uneasy about it, but what can I truly say about it? I begin to tell him my good news about my job. He had no enthusiasm in his voice and told me he will call me back. I looked at my phone as the call ended, not believing he hung up on me. Shaking my head in disbelief I started to walk to the train, texting Yanza at the same time to see where she was and to ask if I can use her car tonight. I didn't receive a text back until after I got off the train at Midtown; she said she was home and that she has a show tonight, but we will talk further about it when I get home. "Okay," I texted back.

When I got off the train and began to walk home, I started to think about Keith again. I understand and respect that he's a star athlete at his school while managing to keep his GPA high, but I believe a person makes time for what they really want to make time for. As I walked, thoughts after thoughts consumed me. It's said the mind is the devil's playground, and that a simple thought can ruin a person's spirit. In my case my spirit is not ruined but it is a little broken.

I tried to shake the thoughts out of my head as I entered the apartment.. I didn't want Yanza to see me looking worried and start asking questions. Besides, there are more important matters at hand.

I walked in and greeted Yanza as she was running around like a chicken with her head cut off.

"Hey, is everything alright? What are you looking for," I asked.

"Hey, I'm sorry, I'm looking for my black and red camel toe heels. I need them for tonight," she said back to me.

"They are in my closet, remember? You loan them to me over the weekend," I reminded her.

She went to go get them as I laid out on the couch in the living room. I was a little tired from the day, but I had no time to relax because I had to find a ride to the show.

Yanza walked back in with the shoes in her hands and went to put them in her model bag. Suddenly it then clicked that she did say she had a show on tonight. I called her into the living room to ask her where her show was held. She responded back at The H Lounge. I started to grin from ear to ear while she stood there looking confused. I told her what happened to me at work today and about my trial base temporary promotion. She was excited for me more so than my own boyfriend was. We further talked about us riding together to the show and the time that we will have to leave. I agreed to it all and went to go get ready.

A few hours later and we were on our way to the show. I was feeling some type of way because I hadn't heard back from Keith. As we drove I tried to not show my annoyance because I didn't want to ruin the mood, this was a big moment for me and I was prepared to do a great job.

When we got to the show Yanza jumped out and ran back stage because she was running a little behind. Since I still had some time to kill before the show started I decided to pull out my phone and call Keith. He picked up as I was about to hang up.

"Hey bae, how are you doing?" he said, sounding out of breath.

It took a moment for me to respond back because everything caught me off guard. "I'm doing good, excited about my new trial position," I said, "What are you doing?"

He fumbled over his words as he tried to answer the question. He said that he was at a last call practice but the feeling I was having now stated otherwise.

I tried to ask more questions, but he rushed me off the phone saying Corey was calling before hanging up again. I looked at the phone to see if he really just hung up on me again. He must have forgotten who I was before I met him. My blood was boiling. 0-80, my temperature rose but I knew I had to calm myself because I will not let that fool ruin tonight. I looked at the clock as I was doing a little breathing exercise I used to do back in my Laquesha Johnson days. It was time for me to meet Journey at the front entrance. I got out of the car and begin my walk around to the front. I didn't spot him as I was approaching the front entrance.

"How's he going to tell me not to be late and he was," I muttered to myself.

I looked around and still did not see him but I spotted Corey, so I walked over to him.

"Hey Corey, I should've known you were going to be here," I said to him with a friendly smile.

"I got to support my girl. She is going to be big one day," he replied smiling.

"I wish I had someone to support me," I said sadly.

"He does, he's just busy with school and track."

"Yeah and another girl," I said darkly.

"Do you really believe that," Corey asked.

"I really don't know what to believe anymore with him." I spoke those words just as Journey was walking up to me out of breath.

"Hey Tina, I apologize for being late. Are you ready for tonight?" he asked.

"I'm nervous," I said.

Journey started giving me advice to calm down and relax. He had me laughing forgetting that Corey was standing there until he gave me this strange look that quickly brought me back to my senses. I introduced Journey to Corey, they were pleasant but I could tell that Corey was on defense.

After the pleasantry, we made our way into the show. Because Journey and I were covering it we were assigned to sit in the front row. Corey was asked to sit with us by Journey and he happily accepted because it beats sitting in the back where he usually sits.

The lights got dim as the announcer came on to hype the crowd up for the show. After about five minutes of his comedic that had everyone in tears he introduced the first artist to perform before the models. It was a trio of young ladies performing an original song. By the middle of their performance, people were standing and applauding. They owned the stage in my opinion; I would sign them.

The fashion show lasted for about two hours. The whole show was well put together. I took notes as I watched Journey interview a few models.

"Are you ready to do your first face to face interview Tina," he asked.

"No," I said.

"You can do it. It's no different then the phone interviews you do."

"Them standing in front of me is a big difference."

He gave me the liberty to choose the model I would like to interview. I looked around and spotted Yanza. I walked up to her and introduced myself and asked if I could interview her. Even though she was my girl I was nervous because it was my first time and she was so professional. I could tell she was trying to make me feel at ease, but it wasn't working.

By the end of the night I was feeling accomplished because I got through it. Journey was informing me of my next steps and what we were to be doing tomorrow while I waited for Yanza and Corey to come out. I felt like I was made for this position. Everything he was telling me I was confident in knowing that I can do the job and do it well. Yanza and Corey finally approached us, creeping like they were trying to listen in on the conversation Journey and I were having. Yanza was giving me a look like, "girl what are you doing." I just smiled back at her.

Journey began to talk with Yanza about the show telling her how great she was. She thanked him humbly but I could tell she was trying not to get a big head about it. Corey was starting to feel some type of way because to him Journey was being too friendly. I caught the signs and drew his attention back toward me. We continued conversing about the show until Corey was ready to go. Journey mentioned that it was getting late and that he will see me tomorrow at work.

Journey started to head towards his car, Corey, Yanza, and I heading towards theirs.

"Girl, I see what was going on there, Journey is trying to explore his writings of you," Yanza burst out.

"Don't let Keith find out," said Corey chiming in. That just made my mood turn sour. "

"Keith? I haven't heard from your friend since he hung up on me! Look it's almost eleven o'clock and there's been no call or text! If this had been a job he would have been fired."

When I regained my composure, I saw the looks that Corey and Yanza were giving me.

"Calm down Tina, we're sorry we brought him up," Corey said.

I said nothing and walked to get into Yanza's car. She walked behind me and asked if I was okay. I nodded yes without looking at her. She then asked if I was able to drive home because she wanted to ride with Corey.

"Okay, " I said before jumping into the driver's seat. Corey came over and told me their plans for the night and asked me if I wanted to join.

"No." I declined. I just wanted to go and lay it down for the night.

The night was calm, peaceful here in the city. I walked into the apartment to nothing but silence. I checked my phone and still no call or text from my so-called boyfriend. I locked it and threw it on the dresser as I walked into my room. I sat on my bed and grabbed my poetry book. Alone, lost, and confused, I began to write

A breath of silence; listen and you can hear the world tremble
under the presents of the giant. The face that appeals in the mist
is that of the child crying out for salvation. The sound of the voice
is choked because it is claustrophobic, surrounded by the wills of man.
With hope far from sight, it surrenders and gives up the ghost with

the prayer to be rebirth into a new spirit.

*Soulless enemies emerge, taking away
the faith and renaming it fear.
Cast out into the darkness, the guilt
succumbs to the pain to show
invisible bruises. The skin becomes
tainted, unbearable to wear; but
wearing it is the curse for not believing.
The light is at a distant, like Pluto
is to the sun, the cold is always felt but
the warmth is the desire.*

*On a platform not knowing which brick
road to take, wishing Dorothy would
lend me Glinda, for just one moment to
guide me home. The world is vast,
infinite in size but the ant always knows
the right route to clear the danger.
Brave hearts stand forth but with no
soul the heart is forced to stand still
while the battle escapes and wither off
into another dimension.*

Coffee House
Chapter 3

The next morning I woke up refreshed with a new sense of security. I was confident to know that I will get the new position. Later, as I walked into work with a little pep in my step, I spotted Journey; he looked at me and smiled and before making his way over to me.

"Well now look at you, you must have hit the lottery or something because you are glowing."

"No, just feeling good today. I guess I woke up on the right side of the bed this morning," I responded."

"Well good," charging the tone of his voice. "It's time to start on this article about the show last night," he said, sounding more stern as he headed to his office with me following."

Upon me entering he said it took you long enough. Right there is where I was taken out of my happy-go-lucky mood and Laqueisha Johnson spoke up.

"Hold up because I think you have your people confused," I said as I walked over to the table to free my hands up. "I'm not the one to be playing mind games with or in your case trying to play mind games on. I don't know if you are bi-polar or have a split personality, but this chick right here is not the one. So let me set the record straight…"

He just burst out laughing before I could finish what I was saying like I was just amusing him.

"Are you serious right now? You know what, I don't have time for this," I said as I turned to grab my things and started for the door to leave the office.

"Wait, wait wait," he said trying to contain his laughter. "I'm sorry, come sit down."

I flipped my hair as I turned back around getting out of my ghetto mood. He got me messed up!

He got up still trying to contain his laughter to escort me to my seat. I declined his offer and walked myself to my seat. I listened as he explained to me his behavior was a test to determine if I was a push over or not. Continuing, he explained that the aggression that I'd displayed I'd need as a field agent.

"Things won't always be as smooth as it was at the fashion show," he said to me. I shook my head in agreement and we began the review from last night.

We looked over the pictures that were taken to see which ones we were going to put in the magazine. After we selected the photos, we were able to write up the articles and use the interviews to quote the models. The entire process lasted the whole day.

Our rough copy was delivered to the editorial team for approval. I smiled because I know I had this position. I began to gather my things to head out. Journey followed and engaged me in a conversation. All I wanted to do was go catch my train, get home, and dive into bed.

"I'll admit, you did a good job today. And I agree with the boss your writing is poetic. Do you write poetry," he asked?

"In my spare time I do."

"By the way you write here I know it's good. Do you ever showcase your work, because I would love to be the audience," he said with a smile.

"...and I can see you are a smooth talker, but to answer your question no I don't. My work is for my eyes only."

"Interesting, maybe you should," he said as he walked out of the office.

"How are you going to end a conversation like that," I said as he continued out the door. What was so interesting?

I hurried to gather the reminder of my things before running after him. As I step out of the office he's standing there waiting.

"Now where could you be going in such a rush," he asked with a smile.

I was a deer caught in headlights. I had to think of something because I didn't want him thinking I was chasing after him.

"I was heading to catch my train before I missed it," I said, stuttering over my words.

He just started laughing. I was trying to convince him that what I said was the truth, but he wasn't believing me.

"So you're going to act like that? You're just going to walk away," he said as I was walking for the door. "Ok hold up," I heard him.

He caught up to me outside of the building. He grabbed my hand to stop me but it sent chills up my arm. I'd never felt that from anyone before.

"Hey I'm sorry, I was just clowning with you," he said to me looking innocent.

I just exhaled deeply.

"You alright," he asks.

I couldn't say anything so I just responded with a head nod. He asked again and nothing was said. He asked again and still I said nothing. Suddenly, he grabbed my shoulders and I felt light headed. My legs felt weak. He caught me as I collapsed to the ground.

"You're not riding the train today," he said while helping me up and directing me towards his car.

Next thing I remember was waking up in my room with Yanza putting a cold cloth over my fourhead.

"What happened," I asked, trying to get my eyes adjusted to the lighting in my room.

"You fainted, Journey brought you home," said Yanza.

"How are you feeling," said Journey as he came to sit next to me on the bed.

I just looked at him then, to Yanza before looking back at him. I snivel out, I feel better. I looked back up at Yanza because she was giving me that look, the same look she gave me at the show. Looking at Journey, she smiled and excused herself.

Alone Journey dadded the cloth on my head, "you scared me for a minute there. I never had that happen to me."

I smiled at him and said I never had this happen to me before either.

An hour had passed with just Journey and I laughing and talking, mostly about the job and position, and Yanza walking in checking on me from time to time, giving me that gigantic smile every time Journey is not looking.

Things were at peace, more so poetic until I heard a voice that I hadn't heard in quite a while. Keith came charging into my room, stopping in his tracks at the door when he saw Journey sitting next to me on my bed. "What is this? Who are you," he asked accusingly.

"What good, I'm Journey Rivers. Tina and I work together," he said, extending his hand. "She wasn't feeling well so I brought her home." "And you are?"

"I'm her boyfriend," Keith said, and I just rolled my eyes because he has not been much of that in the past few months.

"Glad to finally meet you. Tina has been speaking highly of you," Journey said leaving me looking confused.

They continued small talk back and forth. I figured out what Journey was doing by saying I talk about Keith all the time. After a while Keith became more at ease.

"Well it's about time to take my leave," said Journey. "Good to meet you Keith; and Tina I'll see you at work."

After Journey leaves Keith and I stare at each other in silence. I didn't have anything to say to him. He tries to say something but I cut him off and say that he can just go ahead and follow Journey right out the door. He looks at me shocked like I was speaking to him in a foreign language. I repeated, "...and you can just follow him right out the door." Keith started to walk over closer to me. He looked at my bed and then went for the chair at my desk. He pulled it over to sit in it.

"Since you can't understand the words I'm speaking and excuse yourself from my presence, I'll just have to excuse myself from yours," I said to him.

I got up from my bed only to be met by the arms of Keith and him yelling out to Yanza for help. I heard footsteps in the distance rapidly getting closer to my room. I heard Yanza yelling out "Tina" and Keith saying, "go call 911" before my eyes began to get heavy and I went out.

Coffee House
Chapter 4

I laid in darkness, my surroundings unfamiliar to me. I heard a voice in the light calling and asking me to come forth. The light was warm and peaceful, welcoming. I extended my hand out towards it accepting the invitation.

I became air, flowing freely, my feet no longer touching the surface they were on. I was being pulled towards the light. I wasn't afraid, nor did I question what was on the other side. If anything, I just allowed the angelic force to take me.

As I continued to get closer to the light, the voice in the light became clearer and more familiar. "Daddy is that you," I called out. But no answer was sent back. A tear fell from my eye down my cheek. I hadn't heard my father's voice in so long; he passed away when I was only ten. I remember sitting on his lap on the front porch of our house. He used to tell me that no matter what happens, or where I end up in life, he will always be there for me. At that time, I didn't know that he had stage four cancer. I didn't understand what cancer was, but it took him away from me. The closer I came towards the light, the more my father's voice became clearer, the more I cried.

His face then appealed to me without the light. With my hand still extended I tried to touch his face. I began to call out to him saying "daddy, daddy I miss you so much. Daddy I need you." Upon saying that, my father's face transformed into the face of Journey, and the light engulfed me as I whispered out his name.

I awoke to Keith saying "I need you. Please don't leave me." I opened my eyes as they adjusted to the light. I began to search the room to see where I was at. Keith walked away from me and Yanza and Corey came running up.

"Thank God you're awake," Yanza exclaimed!

"Where am I," I asked weakly.

"You're in the hospital. You were in a coma for two weeks," Yanza told me.

"What happened? How? My job?" I asked, throwing question after question.

"Calm down Tina," said Yanza. "the doctors really don't know what's going on with you, and your job is fine. Journey made sure of that."

Hearing his name sent chills through me. Why was this happening to me?

"Where's Keith," I asked, realizing he wasn't in the room anymore.

"We don't know, he just walked out, but he was here every day. He never left your bedside."

The nurse walked into the room to check my vitals. Everything was fine according to the monitors, but it couldn't be. After the nurse left, Yanza asked Corey to go down to the café to get us some food. After Corey left Yanza looked at me.

"What it is," I asked her.

She looked at me for what felt like a few minutes before she started to speak.

"Keith does love you Tina," she said, "He cried everyday, praying to God you recover. He started to reminisce on when his brother was in the hospital, and how he almost lost him, and now he almost lost you. He never left your side; talking to you everyday, thinking that you would hear his voice and follow it back to him."

"So why does he treat me the way that he does? Why all the secrets," I asked her.

"He talked with me about it, and about the things that were happening over the past two weeks. He was waiting for you to wake up to explain everything."

"Well I'm here, I'm up. I'm okay according to the monitors, and he leaves," I said feeling a bit frustrated.

Yanza looked at me and exhaled, "Tina when you woke, you called out Journey's name," she said to me.

"I don't believe that. I couldn't have." I said in disbelief.

She said nothing, she just left me to my thoughts. I didn't know if I should call Keith or not. I picked the phone up only to put it back down.

Moments later Corey came back in with the food followed by the doctor. The doctor went over my test results. The doctor reaffirmed what the nurse had stated earlier, "your test results came back as normal as possible. You are as healthy as can be, but we would like to keep you to monitor you for a few days to be on the safe side," he explained to me. "How do you feel."

I told him I felt fine. I guess a little sleep was all I really needed. He smiled. I continued to tell him that I was okay to leave even though he insisted I stay for monitoring. After a while we both agreed that I was able to leave tomorrow, but if I felt any pain, or slept longer than 10 hours at a time, to come back immediately. He also told Yanza and Corey to monitor my behavior, which they both agreed to.

As soon as the doctor had left, Yanza and Corey started in on the questioning. They both asked if I was sure I made a good decision. I told them yes and that nothing was wrong with me. They disagreed, but it was my decision. I then asked about Keith again. Corey said that he had called him on his way to the café to get the food. "He said he was tired and was heading to the crib to go to sleep and that he was turning his phone off." I feel some type of way about that, but I didn't want to start anything.

The next day, I was ready to leave the hospital. The nurse had me sign my discharge papers and gave me instructions on monitoring my behavior. I skimmed over the paperwork before I signed to make sure I wasn't signing my life away.

I was able to walk but the nurse insisted that I was wheeled out. Corey had pulled the car around to the front entrance. Finally! I was ready to leave this place; to go talk with Keith. I had to explain things to him as best I could.

The entire ride to Yanza's and my apartment was in silence. I was lost in thought going back and forth with thoughts of Journey and Keith. I loved Keith with my heart but his distance had made room for another to enter. I had to talk to him to try and explain, but how and where do I start? I don't fault Keith for leaving after he heard what escaped my mouth at the hospital but I can fault him for his secrets and absences.

We arrived at my home and I got out of the car on my own. Corey and Yanza insisted that I allow them to help me, but I was capable of doing it on my own. I continued to walk to the front door and proceed to open it. I grabbed my chest as I stood like a deer caught in the headlights, gasping for air. Corey and Yanza dropped whatever they had in their hands and came charging over to me, asking if I were alright?

"Yeah I'm fine. I just thought my surprise coming home party was on the other side of this door. A girl hasn't been here in two weeks," I joked.

All they could do was say that I was too much and shook their heads as they walked back to pick up the things they'd dropped.

I walked in the apartment with thoughts of Keith on my mind. I needed to talk with him. I went for my phone when the door opened and Journey appeared..

"What are you doing here," I asked harshly.

"Well it's good to see you too Tina," he responded. "I take it I'm not the person you wanted to see?"

"It's not that it's just..." I said, pausing to collect my thoughts. I can't tell him anything close to my feelings. "It's just complicated," I admitted.

"Oh I get it, the boyfriend. No need to explain. I stopped at the hospital but was told you were discharged. I hurried here to inform you that you got the promotion. I figured some good news is what you needed after what you've been through. Mr. Kobe was impressed with your work, and he hopes you get well soon."

I was overjoyed. I was ready to dive into it. Maybe it would clear my mind of the negatives of my life. "When can I return," I asked.

"If you're up for it I will see you in the office tomorrow," he said as he exited.

"Are you crazy, you can't go to work tomorrow! You just got out of the hospital, you need to rest," Yanza yelled at me.

"I've rested for two weeks according to you, Corey, and the doctor, so rest is the last thing I need."

"You are talking foolishly Tina!"

"Yeah said the girl who took her boyfriend back after he cheated on her with a 50 year old woman!"

"Girl," Yanza said, calming down exhaling. "That was love, something you know nothing about since you can't keep your eyes on your man and off... Journey," she said walking off into her room.

"What's going on in here," Corey said, walking in from outside with more things from the car.

"Nothing Corey! Have you heard from Keith," I asked.

"Not since the call at the hospital. Where is Yanza?"

I pointed towards her room and he went off to her. I needed to get out of here. I've been caged for too long. I gather my things and my thoughts and headed out the door. I had no destination on where I was going. I just started to walk. I approached the transit station and decided to get on it. I flipped a coin to see rather I was going to head north or south. South won it.

The train arrived and I got on it still not knowing where I was going. I rode a few stops and got off. I couldn't take the Atlanta gossip any longer. I just wanted it to be silent. I walked out of Five Points station feeling defeated from my day. I thought maybe some entertainment in the Atlanta Underground would help my mood but there was nothing going on there so I was left walking around with no destination.

I was lost in my thoughts. The night sky was blind in a sheet of gray. A cool gentle breeze was beginning; it felt like a storm was developing. I needed to get home before a downpour began. I felt a single drop on my shoulder and I knew I needed to get to a bus stop quickly. It's funny how the Atlanta's weather is. You can feel the phrases of all four seasons in the course of a week. The rain fall was beginning and I was still too far from the bus stop. My day was in shambles, and now my night heading the same way.

I reached the bus. I stopped and looked at the schedule to see when the next bus would arrive and it won't arrive any time soon. I looked at my surroundings to survey the area, not all of this city is a good place to be after dark. I realize that I was not too far from Corey and Keith's house. I thought maybe I should go by there and wait out the storm. At least I'll be at a safe and dry on the porch if he doesn't let me in.

It had begun to pour harder just as I reached Keith's porch. I hesitated ringing the bell because I was afraid to face him, but the rain made it cold and I knew I couldn't stay out here for too long. I rung the bell, and after a few moments he opened the door. We stood face to face staring at each other in the eye.

"What are you doing here," he said angrily.

"I just wanted to get out of the rain," I said.

"Journey not available?"

I said nothing, I just followed him into the house.

"You can wait here. Have you called someone to pick you up?"

I shook my head no.

"Well do so, and fast," he said, "You can use my phone if you don't have yours."

"I was wondering if we could talk," I said meekly.

He stopped in his tracks, and not looking at me he said, "you shouldn't wonder. Just tell your ride to hurry up."

"Keith, it's getting boring in here," a voice said coming from his room.

"Is that...who is that Keith," I asked harshly.

"You don't get to question me anymore," he said as he walked into his room, slamming the door behind him.

Just then tears began to stream down my face; why did I come here? This was a mistake! I had no one to call because Yanza was upset with me from our fight earlier, something I was so out of line for. On top of that she's with Corey. Instead, I dialed up one person I hoped would be able to help me out right now. He answered on the first ring; after telling him my situation he asked me the address and told me he'd be here shortly. All the while Keith remained in his room with whomever was in there.

After a while I heard a car pull up, looking out, I could see it was Journey. So, with one final look at Keith's room I ran out into the rain and jumped in. After I got in, he started peppering me with questions, asking what happened. Him asking made me wish I would've stayed in the rain so he couldn't see me crying. Xscape's song "In The Rain" made perfect sense to me now and it played over and over in my mind. I didn't want to talk about my situation with him, so I remained quiet the entire ride and just cried.

When we got back to my apartment, I thanked him for picking me up and told him I'd see him tomorrow.

"Are you sure you want to come in tomorrow? Maybe you sure take a day or two for yourself."

I just repeated to him I'd see him tomorrow and thanked him again for the ride home.

I got out of the car and watched him drove off. For a while I stood out into the rain and let it wash over me. Feeling the bumps on my skin emerging and the flow of the water as it made patterns going down my body, was soothing. I broke out of my moment when a lady came building asking if I was all right. I told her I will be, come morning.

Entering the apartment I heard the moans coming from Yanza's room. At least someone was having a good time tonight. Ignoring them I went into the bathroom to draw myself a warm bath with rose petals and lit some candles. I turned on some music to drown out the noise from my roommate, and poured myself a glass of wine before settling in and just relaxed. When morning comes I will be the number one person in my life.

Chapter 5
Coffee House

Prideful never
Envious to none
Denounced but unstoppable
My stride, a loaded gun

Believe or disbelieve
My tongue bears no despair
The cries of the fallen
Endure the wrath they dare

My ego immense
Embark on a journey, least attend
The queen has arrived

My spirit echos within

I am the force
The past, the present, the future
Compliments the entity inside
Unifying the me, the myself, and the I

I walked into my work feeling unstoppable. I was in Laqueisha Johnson mode, and I made sure everyone knew it. Journey noticed me and made his way over.

"Excuse me, my name is Journey Rivers and you are," he said to me in a serious tone.

I extended my hand and replied, "my name is Laqueisha Johnson, pleasure to meet you." With that he started laughing, not here for it. I walked off to start work.

"Hey," he said walking up from behind me, "what's all this? Are you okay?"

"I am fine. I just have a lot of work to catch up on."

"I understand that, I do," he said "but why are you acting like this? Did something happen last night after I dropped you off?"

"Nothing happened, I just forgot who I was. Now if you'll excuse me.

I walked into Mr. Kobe's office to ask about assignments I can do. He was ending what looked like a meeting with his assistants. As they exit he turned his attention toward me.

"Ms. Mills, this must be important for you to barge into my office."

I said nothing. He was taken aback with my silence.

"How are you feeling Ms. Mills? Journey explained everything. I'm glad to have you back but can take a few days. No need to return so soon."

"Sir," I said, " I appreciate your concern, but I'm here to do a job. Are there any open assignments? I would appreciate that."

He said nothing; I guess he was in shock. He just stared at me before speaking at last. "I see in your absence you've become grim; I have the perfect assignment for you."

He picked up his phone and called Sharon. He instructed her to get the Williamsburg's assignment ready for me.

"I know, but it's more information we need," he said speaking over the phone. "Thank you, Ms. Mills will be right out to collect it from you."

He hung the phone up and told me he wants the assignment done and ready for the editorial team by tomorrow.

"And who am I partnered with?" I asked, standing confidently.

"I'm sure you will be able to handle it alone, but it may be an all-nighter so I hope you had plenty of rest."

"Well I welcome a good challenge," I said tersely as I turned to leave the office.

I headed to Sharon to retrieve the assignment. I looked it over,and then headed to my desk. I ran into Journey again. I don't know why, but he's really starting to get under my skin.

"What is it that you want now," I asked annoyed.

"Look Tina, I really don't know what your problem is, but I told you about bringing your emotions into work. You are going to mess around and lose this job," he said to me.

I rolled my eyes and proceeded to my desk.

"What assignment did he give to you," he asked as he followed me.

As I got to my desk I sat down and handed him the folder I got from Mr. Kobe.

"He gave you the Williamsburg's assignment," he asked, shocked. "Who are you working with?"

"It's just me,"

"Tina, this is career suicide. You are new to this position. You can't mess this up."

"So why don't you stop this game of twenty questions and allow me to get started. I have until sunup to have it completed," I said shot back.

"Fine, I'll be your funeral," he said before walking off.

I watched him walk off before I took a look at everything in front of me. It's a lot to handle for anyone but I'm not just anyone. I was already preparing myself for this all-nighter, all I had to do now was get started.

After I read over the assignment, I'd have to interview representatives of the different companies listed to understand the new developments happening in Atlanta that are removing minorities from their homes. Being that this article is assignmented two pages of the magazine everything must be precise and accurate.

I began making phone calls to the companies to schedule interviews for today. Some of the companies' representatives were not available for a face to face interview but I was allowed to perform a quick phone interview with them.

I was making my arrangements to leave the office, plotting the route I'll be taking to make the travel time more feasible. For a quick second it dawned on me to call Yanza and ask for her car but after the argument we'd last night I decided against it. Public transportation would be fine, besides, with the Atlanta traffic, it's quicker to get around.

I packed up my things and began to head out the door. On the way out I passed Journey's office, he looked at me, shook his head and then continued whatever he was doing.

Stepping outside the office I saw it was a beautiful day; the sun shining but slightly cool. I made my way to the Marta Transit Line to head to my first appointment that's located in the south side of the city. The receptionist informed me that their representative was leaving town later today, so it was a must that I got to them first.

On the train, the ride to the south side was relaxing. I had my headphones in and the world drowned out. I was lost in my world until I got the whiff of a dead dog. I looked up to see a homeless guy asking for money. It always amazes me how they are always asking for change on a transit line that takes money to get on it. I shook my head at the thought and gave him the loose change I had.

As the train got closer to my stop I was feeling good. This was going to be a breeze. I was going to have this article completed by morning and Mr. Kobe wouldn't have any reason not to give me my praises and a raise. A smile slowly began to appear on my face but it was quickly wiped away when I noticed these two girls looking and laughing in my direction. I was like they were having a good time at my expense, but that couldn't be because they didn't know me from a can of paint. I ignored them and continued to escape in my music.

Soon enough their laughter was becoming disruptive to the point where it was starting to interrupt the other passengers. Lequeisha Johnson wanted to shut them up, but I know I couldn't because I was on the job and it wasn't fully directed at me, or so I thought. When we got to their stop, they made it known everything they were doing was aimed at me. Their whispering became clearer and the laughter became more pronounced.

"Yeah girl, that's her, I could tell from the picture," one of the girls said to the other.

The other girl couldn't get her words out because she was laughing so hard. Exiting the train they stared at me until it began moving and I was out of their sight.

"I don't know what that was all about but if it was any other day, they would have been riding shotgun underneath this train," I whispered to myself.

I hurried to regain my composure as the train approached my stop. When it got there I started my walk to the facility. When I got to the front entrance and made my way inside, I was greeted by the receptionist.

"Welcome to Global Connections!"

"Hi, my name is La'Tina Mills and I'm here to see Mr. Culpepper; he's expecting me."

"I'm sorry, but he had to step out sooner than expected but he left this with me to give to you" she said politely as she handed me a folder before continuing, "he apologizes for the inconvenience."

I flipped through the folder quickly before saying... "Thank you, have a nice day," I said before heading to my next appointment.

My other appointments went as well as the first. I met with the companies' representatives and received more information than I could have bargained for. I was on my way north to an office in Sandy Springs. It was getting late, and I had to transfer to the North Springs line, but I still had time. I was scheduled to meet with Mrs. Wahlgren, the head of Community Shared at 8pm. As I was waiting I reached for my phone and saw I had missed calls from Yanza, Corey, Journey, and, surprisingly, Keith. I started to return Yanza's call until I heard the announcer come over the intercom indicating there would be a delay due to single tracking. No! I thought, this couldn't be happening, not now! Everything has been going so well today! I tried calling Mrs. Wahlgren to explain the situation but she didn't. I left a voicemail and hoped I could get there before she left.

I was really starting to get worried because 30 minutes had passed and there was still no train. I dialed up Mrs. Wahlgren again but still no answer. Without a response I had a feeling that Mrs. Wahlgren was already gone; still, I had to go just to make sure.

By the time I arrived at Community Shared it was after 9pm, and the building was dark. Heading back to the train I had to get back to the office to get this article completed before the morning. It was around midnight. My body was exhausted and needed rest, but I had to get this article finished.

A few hours later I was in turmoil trying to piece together the puzzle to get this article together. I was beginning to feel panicked because time was steadily ticking away. It seemed like every time I glanced at the clock 45 minutes to an hour had passed. What I needed was to calm down and focus. Getting up, I walked around for a few minutes to regain my composure. Sitting back down I got back to work.

After a few hours of work I saw that it was close to 6am, dawn was breaking and I was putting the finishing touches on the article. I had just enough time to print and place it on Mr. Kobe's desk. I walked over to the copy room, passing a few of my co-workers that were walking in. We greeted each other but I was in no mood to talk. They were a bit hesitant about speaking because they probably assumed I was still in my Lequeisha Johnson mode. At this point all I wanted to do was hand this article in and head to my crib and crash for a few hours.

After leaving the copy room, I passed Journey as I headed to Mr. Kobe's office.

"How was your night? I called you a few times to check up on you," he said.

"It went well," "I got everything completed. I was just heading to Mr. Kobe's office now to drop it off."

"Well I'm impressed! Hats off to you! I'll admit, I didn't think you could pull it off."

"Well it's a good thing no one pays you to think, now isn't it," I said back to him sarcastically.

As I looked past him in the direction of Mr. Kobe's office, I saw that Mr. Kobe was heading into his office. I wanted to put this article on his desk before he arrived at work to avoid conversation.

"Excuse me Journey; I have to get this article to Mr. Kobe," I said walking past him.

I was able to reach Mr. Kobe just as he was sitting in his chair.

"Good Morning Mr. Kobe, I have The Williamsburg's assignment as you requested," I said, a little excited.

The look that was pasted on his face was priceless. He held out his hand, signaling for me to bring it to him. I proceeded to walk towards him and hand him the article. I turned to walk out so I could finally head home, but he stopped me.

"Wait right there," he said.

I turned back towards him as he was looking over the article. He said nothing as he was skimming through it.

"Sir,"

"I am impressed. I commend you on a job well done," he said, "I will admit that I had my doubts but you got it done."

I looked at him and smirked before saying thank you and motioning to exit.

"Maybe we can put you on a group assignment where you would be the lead," he said.

"That will be fine," I responded, flipping my hair as I turned to exit.

I felt amazing and relieved that I finished the article. I was back in my Lequeisha Johnson mode, and I was feeling fabulous. After leaving my desk, I walked down the center floor with my head held high like I was Tyra Banks on the catwalk. My co-workers were just in envy and whispering amongst themselves but none dared to try and stop me. I walked and sashayed until I spotted Journey in his office. I stopped in his doorway and struck a pose. I was fiercer than Sasha. I was a diva in my own right because I did the impossible. I managed to finish an assignment that required a team, all on my own.

I said nothing to Journey, nor did he say anything to me. The looks that each of us had on our faces said it all. As I turned, I side eyed him and continued to walk out the building. I was met by a glimmer of sun trying to force its way through the clouds. It was a chilly morning.

I tried to wrap myself as warmly as I could to prepare for my walk but nothing was working. The chill of the wind still managed to make its way through my clothes to attack my skin.

"I guess Ms. High and Mighty gets cold too," a voice said coming from behind me followed by a parade of laughter.

I already knew who it was before I even turned around.

"Well you can freeze, or you can allow me to drive you home."

I stopped and thought about it for a second. It was cold and a ride did sound inviting but the awkward silence or the childish game of twenty questions is the con to this pro that I really don't want to part-take in.

I was beginning to walk again when a gust of wind blew and hugged my body sending chill bumps throughout it. I quickly agreed to the ride by dropping my head and turning towards Keith. He walked towards me and put the coat he had on around me. I hesitated at first, but then he said it's cold and all he wanted to do was take me home.

His car was parked right out in front of my office building. We approached his car and it was already running so I knew it was warm inside. He surprised me when he opened the passenger side door for me because it was something he hadn't done in a while.

"Why are you being so nice to me?"

"I'm a nice guy," he said, still holding the car door for me.

I gave him the side eye look as I got in the car nervously. He closed my door and ran to get into the driver side door. He looked at me and smiled,

"Are you getting warm or do you need me to turn the heat up?"

"The heat is okay," I said.

We pulled out the parking space and for the first two minutes of the ride there was silence.

"First of all Keith, how did you know where I was," I asked, finally breaking the silence. He just started to laugh.

"I couldn't get a good morning or a thank you for the ride first?"

"Well good morning and thank you for the ride, now how did you know where I was," I repeated .

"Okay calm down; I know it's cold but you don't have to be," he said with that beautiful smile of his.

"After blowing up your phone to no response. Yanza started calling around to all the hospitals and Corey put out an APB on you, I made the sensible suggestion to locate Journey and he told me where you were and what you were doing. So I chose to pick you up this morning, is that alright with you my lady?"

I looked at him because he hadn't called me that in such a long time. I nodded my head in agreement.

"Good because we are here," he said.

I looked around and said, "here where? This is not my apartment in midtown!"

"I brought you to my house," he said getting out of the car letting all the cold into it.

He walked over to my side of the car and opened the door.

"Why are you being so nice?" I repeated.

He said nothing this time, he just held out his hand to receive mines before escorting me into the house.

When we got into the house I smelled the aroma of food. Keith led me to a table spread with food: grits with cheese, pancakes, eggs, sausages, and bacon with toast spread with strawberry jam.

"A feast fit for a queen," he said, pulling out a chair for me.

"You did all this?"

He nodded his yes before signaling for me to come sit.

"This all looks great but I need a shower first," I said.

"That I figured so I have that ready for you as well," he said.

He walked me to the bathroom and led me in. Inside it was filled with lit candles, soft music, and a bubble bath with rose petals.

"Who are you and what have you done with Keith?"

"He is right here. Journey told me about your job. I knew you were going to be successful with it so I planned all this to celebrate."

"Well I'm glad someone knew I could do it," I said before kissing him.

"Are you joining me?"

"This is all for you ," he said before starting to undress and help me into the tub.

I took off his shirt and pants but only placed his foot in the tub. He started to massage my body starting from my shoulders then to my body. It felt so good. This is what heaven must feel like.

The water is just the right temperature. I splash Keith trying to get him wet so he would get in the tub with me. He splashed me back but got the hint and got in the water with his briefs on. He went from massaging my body to washing me. I couldn't have asked for a better way to celebrate my achievement.

"Thank you for this Keith."

"You're welcome bae."

After about an hour my skin was starting to get wrinkles, so it was time to get out. I know by now the food he prepared was cold, so he just guided me into his bedroom to sleep. I asked him to lay with me and he agreed. He held me as we lay.

"I love you La' Tina Mill," he said.

"I love you too"!

Chapter 6
Coffee House

"Excuse me ma'am. Ma'am," a voice called, waking me up. I looked around to see that Keith was no longer at his house, but back at my desk.

"Are you okay Miss," the voice asked.

I said nothing at first, I just looked up and saw the janitor.

"How did I get here," I asked.

"It looks like you've been here all night. Do you need me to clean that up," he asked pointing to the drool that covered my desk.

"I can get it," I responded embarrassed. "What time is it?"

"It is 6:15am. Are you sure you're okay," he asked looking concerned.

"Yes I'm...oh no the Williamsburg's Assignment, I didn't finish it. I'm so dead," I say panicked because I knew Mr. Kobe would be walking through those doors any minute now.

I began bustling to try and complete much of the assignment as I could before he got in. I thought maybe I could pass it off and Mr. Kobe would be satisfied with that, but why would he from the way I carried on. I thought about calling Journey but I knew because of how I treated him yesterday that he wouldn't come to my rescue.

I was in a panic. Wiping the sweat that was collecting on my forehead trying not to watch the clock. My co-workers began to flood the building. At 8:15, like clockwork, Mr. Kobe walked into the building. In no time he invited me to come to his office in 15 minutes. I know I was dead, by the looks of it ,he knew it too.

I had walked a fine line up until then. I spotted Journey walking in and heading for his office; he saw me, but he said nothing.

I made my way into Mr. Kobe's office and saw that. he was sitting in his chair with his hands cross lending on his chin.

"How are you this morning," he asked. I told him I was okay.

"How was your stay?"

I didn't find anything funny. He held his hand out signaling for me to hand him the completed Williamsburg's Assignment. I walked like a snail to his desk.

"What happened to the spunky upbeat attitude you had yesterday?"

I was boiling because of his taunting. He sat in silence looking over my work. "Is this all you have," he asked.

I said nothing I just stood there glaring at him.

He closed up the folder and sat back in his chair and looked at me. I was getting nervous.

"I am a bit disappointed in this assignment Ms. Mills. I was expecting more out of you," he said. "I can't print this because it would ruin the representation of the magazine."

"It is not that bad sir," I said. "I put my all in that work!"

"This is not what I am looking at," he insisted.

"Well, with the short time frame that I had, and only me working on it..."

"I thought you were able to do anything," he said, getting out of his chair and walking in front of his desk and leaned on it. "I've watched you go from a shy and humble individual to a diva who thinks she owns this magazine. Ms. Mills, I own this magazine. I've received several complaints, but I believed as a field agent, that backbone you have is what a good field agent needs to get the interviews, to get the story. The Williamsburg's Assignment was a test to see how you'd conduct yourself given an assignment that was demanding."

My face dropped on the floor listening to his.

"The Williamsburg's Assignment was completed already. Journey and his team completed it."

I was 52 hot right now. He wasted my time and Journey knew about this. At that time Journey walked in the office with a folder in his hand. He handed it to Mr. Kobe and said nothing.

"This, Ms. Mills, is how the assignment should look when done right," said Mr. Kobe handing a folder to me.

My eyes were bloodshot red. If I was able to cry blood, it would've happened then.

"Why would you have me do all that work yesterday? Do you have any idea of what I went through?"

Neither of them said anything which made Laqueisha Johnson emerge.

"I don't have money to be making false trips for falsework."

I had the Williamsburg's Assignment in my hand and before my eyes all I saw were pieces of it falling to the floor. Mr. Kobe started yelling, but I heard nothing. Journey was looking in shock because of what just happened.

"...and you are fired," said Mr. Kobe, ending his rant. I whipped my hair as I turned to exit his office.

I walked straight to my desk and started packing up my things. Everyone started looking on and making comments trying to figure out what was going on. Finishing packing, I walked straight for the door, not looking at anyone. I was just trying to keep it classy. When I reached the door, I noticed Journey following behind me trying to stop me. I was hoping that Keith was waiting for me like in my dreams but of course he was not.

Journey began running after me yelling for me to stop but I continued to leave. I don't want to hear anything he had to say.

"Tina please," he called.

"What Journey? "You set me up; you all set me up! I don't have anything to say to you!" I said continuing to walk.

"I apologize, but you had this coming,"

As soon as he said that I stopped in my tracks, turned and stared at him. "I had this coming, no one deserved to be handled like the way you and your boss handled me."

"And there it is! What is her name again, Laqueisha Johnson, that's what got you into this situation! You need to shut that ego down and grow up! Whenever something doesn't go your way you have a tantrum. Then the fact that you gave it a name makes it worse. Yes Mr. Kobe set this entire thing up, but I tried to warn you yesterday and you didn't want to listen!"

"You don't know my story Journey!"

"And you don't know mine! When people look at you they don't see your story, all they see is you and the impression you make."

"Well I don't need them. I need no one."

"Well clearly that's not true, evidence proven."

"I don't have time for this," I said walking away from him."

"So what are you going to do now, run like you ran from Carolina," he shouted as I walked away crying.

I didn't know where to go but I knew I needed to be held. My mind though about Keith and that dream. I wondered if he was home. I knew it's early, but I prayed he was home.

I made it to Keith's house in no time. The tears on my face had long since dried, leaving streaks behind. Walking up I cleaned my face before I knocked on the door. I knocked about six times before he answered.

He was shocked to see me standing at his front door this time of morning, but that quickly turned into concern when he saw the look on my face.

"Tina, are you okay? What's wrong," he asked.

Before I could say anything I heard a female's voice in the background. I pushed the door open to see a girl walking out of the guest room with a pajama suit on. She looked at me with a stink look; looking at her I noticed it was the same girl I saw on the train talking about me with her friend.

"You gotta be kidding me," I said.

"It's not a joke boo boo," she yelled at me.

"Tyneisha chill with that," he said to her before turning back to me, "Tina, it's not what you think!"

"It's exactly what you think," yelled Tyneisha.

"I don't have time for this," I said as I dropped the box I had and walked away.

"Tyneisha get your trifling self out my house," I heard Keith say as he ran after me tripping and falling down the steps.

"Tina stop please, let me explain!"

"Just leave me alone Keith."

"No, you need to stop being stubborn and let me explain!"

"Explain what Keith! How I finally understand the truth about you, about us. I saw her and her friend yesterday on Marta. They were talking about me to my face and I couldn't understand why because I never saw them before, but I understand now. I understand perfectly Keith."

"No you don't," Keith said, blooded up from his fall.

"What don't I understand," I asked angrily.

"You don't understand this situation. You don't even know the reason why Tyneisha was here."

"Let me see if I can put the pieces together so I can understand a little better. You spend an uncanny amount of time with her. She is talking about me. She is staying over at your house. You ever feel comfortable enough around her to walk around half naked. So what is it that I don't understand?"

"Have you even heard the saying believe none of what you hear and only half of what you see?"

"Don't taunt me Keith, and that's not how that saying goes."

"I'm sorry bae, but it's cold out here and my body hurts, so can we please go inside and talk," said Keith, giving me the sad puppy dog face. "

No Keith, I just want to go home and sleep," I said.

"You can sleep inside, besides you at least owe me that after you called out Journey's name at the hospital."

"That was a mistake."

"Oh, so it was a mistake that you were falling for him and that every time he's around you, chills shoot through your body? Was all that a mistake?"

"Keith it wasn't what..."

"Hey let's just go inside and talk. It's obvious that we have a lot to talk about."

He was right, we needed to talk. I took his lead and followed him into the house.

When we got back to the porch Keith picked my things up and brought them inside. I took Keith to the bathroom to help him clean up. He wanted to talk about everything after we were done, but I felt my body shutting down. All I wanted was sleep.

"Keith, I know you want to talk, but I'm tired. I've had a long day and night at the office. Can we sleep first and then talk?"

He agreed and held me as we fell asleep.

I had woken up feeling drained like I had been hit by a bus. My eyes were so heavy that I could barely hold them open. I started to lay back down and go back to sleep when I noticed something was strewn over the bed. I rose up to see rose petals spread everywhere. I was in awe, especially when I noticed the entire room: There were flowers everywhere. The candles that were lit were glowing against the night sky.

The music that played softly eliminated the background.

 "Welcome back to the land of the living," said Keith entering the bedroom with a tray of food in his hands. "You slept all day."

 "I must still be dreaming because this is surreal." I said pitching myself to see if I was awake or not.

 "How are you feeling," Keith asked.

 "I'm feeling better. I can't believe you did all this. I literally had a dream like this the other day."

 "Well that dream has nothing on the real thing. Here, eat this, I know you're hungry," he said, placing the tray of food onto my lap. "It smelled so good." One thing about Keith is that he knows how to cook, when he wants too.

 "Thank you, Keith," I said as I began to eat the food he prepared.

 Eating, I savored every bite. Keith was sitting there beside me giving a hungry dog look. I started to feed him some of the food that he prepared. Things could not have been any perfect at this time I thought.

 Just then I remembered that Yanza and Corey had been blowing up my phone for the past few days. I began looking around for my phone so I could call them.

 "What's wrong bae," Keith asked looking at me strangely.

 "My phone, I need to call Yanza."

"No worries, I already took care of it. I called them while you were asleep to let them know you were here and that you are okay. They both were going crazy worrying about you because they thought something happened to you. They'll be over soon." After he said that I was relieved because I knew how Yanza could be.

I couldn't help but think that Keith was beginning to remind me of the old Keith, the one I used to know before all the fighting.

"What's wrong, Why you looking at me like that," Keith asked.

"I'm just so happy right now. After the last couple days, it's good to know that you still care about me."

"I don't just still care Tina, I love you. I never stopped loving you. Yeah, I know the past few years I've been distant because of school and track and the fighting between us, but I never stopped loving you."

"Tina, listen to me," Keith said as he grabbed my hands, "When you were in the hospital I wouldn't leave your side because I was afraid that I was going to lose you. Then when you woke up and called out Journey's name and the fear turned into reality because I lost you."

I just sat there listening to him, tears forming in my eyes because tears were falling from his.

"Tina, you have become my best friend. Because of you, I was able to get through me shooting my brother. Because of you, I was able to escape your brother. You waited for me when my family had to go into hiding. Tina, you move to Atlanta to be with me. That kind of love you don't let die. So, I was planning a surprise for you and Tyneisha was helping me, but I did not know she was throwing shade and dragging your name in the street. I'm so sorry about that bae."

I didn't know what to say.

"I have to ask you something even though I'm afraid of the answer."

"Keith, no I have not slept with Journey," I said before he could get the question out, "But have you and Tyneisha," I asked.

"I'm going to be real with you..."

And with that my head dropped and I released his hands.

"Listen baby please. After I left the hospital, I was hurt. My heart was bleeding. I called Tyneisha and she came to comfort me. That night I was drinking and I was crying in her lap. During the night, things got heated. She kissed me and I didn't fight it. She began to undress and then she began to undress me. At that moment I couldn't go further. All I could think about was you. So we held each other and fell asleep, and that's all that happened I promise."

"That's still not a good reason to do what you did Keith," I said getting up off the bed and walking over to look out the window.

"I know bae, but I was hurting, and I just wanted the hurt to go away and you're not all innocent in this," he said walking over to me.

"I never said I was, but I didn't kiss anyone," I said walking past him heading for the door.

Keith caught up to me, grabbed me and threw me back on the bed. "You're not going anywhere, not this time," he flirtatiously.

"Get off me Keith," I teased.

"No, I love you," he said while getting on top of me.

"Get off me Keith," I said.

"No, he said while kissing my neck.

"Keith!"

"I love you Tina."

"Keith..." was the last thing I got out before his lips met mine.

Chapter 7
Coffee House

"Good Morning Bae! How did you sleep?" Keith asked as I was waking from another good night's rest.

It had been a week since I was fired from my job, and I missed it a lot because it was the one thing I was great at.

"I slept like an angel as always." I responded back to him.

"That's my baby. I cooked breakfast, if you're hungry."

"Thank you. I will be there in a few after I freshen up."

He came to kiss me on my forehead and said okay and to take my time. He said that he was going to keep the food warm.

Keith had become my knight in shining armor again. The person that had saved me from a life of solitude. The life where I had to look over my shoulder in fear that someone would use me to take revenge on my brother because of his extracurricular activity. I felt loved again. I felt wanted again. The things that I longed for because I was practically raised by my brother after my father passed.

I laid in the bed a minute longer just to reminisce on all the things that I had been through in my life up until now. I even thought more about the conversation between me and Keith over the past week. I tried to find fault in others as to why my life is the way it is; to why Laquesha Johnson was even created. But it was no one's fault but my own. She was my backbone, my defense mechanism. She would come to my rescue whenever I felt threatened. That's how I was taught, not to be weak, not to be a pushover. I was not able to be the kind of person my brother wanted me to be so I created my alter-ego. She made me respected, or feared. I didn't care back then because to me respect and fear were one in the same.

People would listen to you regardless. I made my brother proud, but at the end of the day I felt terrible. That was my life until Keith walked in with my brother and his friends.

He seemed broken and a little uncomfortable, but that's how we connected, because I felt the same way. For me, it was love at first sight. I saw a glow in his eye that drew me to him. It made me weak. My brother saw this and didn't approve. But the heartless, unruly, controlling leader he wanted me to be, emerged up against him and wasn't backing down. I wanted Keith, and in return Keith wanted me, and nothing or no-one was going to stop that. My Brother had no choice but to accept it, even though he never did. That's why he wanted Keith to do the unthinkable so he would have been set up and locked away from me. But Keith's heart spoke up, and he didn't go through with the ordeal. He escaped that test he was faced with. He also escaped my brother when he came after him and his family. He was placed into protective custody and was able to complete school.

In all that he never forgot about me, he came and convinced me to move to Atlanta with him and the others. I didn't want to come at first, but what was left for me in Carolina? My mother left, my father passed away, and my brother was in jail until Jesus returned, maybe longer. My Great Aunt, who I was living with, told me to go because I was young and it was time for me to start living, and I did just that.

Besides ,Keith, Corey, and Yanza, moving to Atlanta was the best thing that happened to me.

"Hey bae, Corey and Yanza are here and they are like vultures eating up the food. Are you okay? Why are you crying?" Keith said walking into the room.

I said nothing. I was just looking into his eyes, the same eyes I first fell in love with. Without saying a word, he came and held me.

I was happy. I was beyond happy.

"Keith, thank you for everything. Especially for saving me from myself."

"Tina, it was you who saved me. Who knows where I would be right now if you weren't there telling me how crazy I was for thinking your brother and his friends were the family I needed."

I just started laughing at that comment.

"Why you laughing at that?"

"Because you were crazy for being their errand boy," I said, still laughing.

"Is that what you thought of me?"

"Yes, but I also thought it was cute."

"I hear you." he said smiling, "but come on, let's go eat before Yanza and Corey eat all the food.

"Okay, because I'm going to need it. I've decided to go to the office and apologize to Journey and Mr. Kobe, and I would rather do it on a full stomach."

"I'm glad, and I'll go with you."

"You don't have to."

"I know Tina, but I want to," he said kissing me. "I love you."

The fun at the table was energetic. The four of us were joking, laughing, reminiscing. I apologized to Yanza about the things I said to her. She accepted without hesitation. She even asked when I was coming back home because she kind of missed me being there. Corey wasn't complaining about it though, he liked that he had Yanza to himself so he can do all the freaky and romantic stuff she tells me he does.

The morning was racing away, and I knew I had to get myself together to get to the office. I was praying that everything went smoothly, and that they accept my apology and we move on. I wasn't expecting to get my job back, but apologizing was just something I needed to do. Today was the start of a new day for me and I wanted to start it off right. Laquesha Johnson had been laid to rest.

The car ride there was in silence, nothing but the radio was playing on low. I was trying to figure out what I was going to say because I had no clue. I hadn't heard from Journey this whole week, so I knew he was over me.

Arriving at the office, my stomach was in knots. Maybe eating as much as I did may not have been a good idea because I was feeling like I was going to vomit.

"Baby relax, it's going to be alright," Keith said comforting me. "I'll be right here when you return." He said before kissing my lips relaxing me.

"Thank you, Keith."

I got out of the car and proceeded to walk towards the entrance. My knees buckled a little but I was able to keep my balance. I looked back to see if Keith noticed, and of course he did. He mouthed to me "you got this."

Upon my entrance, everyone just stopped and stared and then the gossip began. I heard everything from here she is Miss all high and mighty to the Diva had returned. Some others were questioning my being here. I ignored them all and continued to Mr Kobe's office.

I passed Journey's office and he just looked shocked. I knew he was also wondering why I was there. I simply nodded at him as to speak, and then continued on my way.

When I approached his door, I could hear him arguing with someone. Great I thought, he's already in a bad mood, but still, I came here for a reason.

I began to lightly knock on the door.

"Come in!"

I nervously opened the door and entered his office. He looked at me as he continued to yell at the person who was on the other end of a call.

"Well I stand by what I said. It's not going to be printed into the magazine! Good day to you." he said, concluding the call and turning his attention to me. "My assistants allowed you to just walk into my office! I'll have to have a word with them, but Ms. Mills, why are you here?"

"321, 123," I counted to myself to keep Laqueisha Johnson from emerging. "I am not here for my job, even though I miss it. I'm just here to apologize for my behavior last week. It was childish and unprofessional of me.

"I agree." he replied.

I waited for more, but he said nothing else.

"Is that all," I asked him.

"It is supposed to be more? What did you expect by coming here today? Apologizing is big of you, but let's not forget about the events that took placed here, and I'm not just speaking about last week. It was a good thing Journey had everything backed up on his computer."

"Yes sir, I understand."

"Good, and with that you can leave my office," he commanded.

I turned to leave but my feet were like they were glued to the floor. I couldn't move.

"Is there a reason why you're still in my office Ms. Mills?"

"Actually it is. you're sitting there all high and mighty like you had nothing to do with what happened. Yes, I admit that I behaved immaturely, but you sir, with all do respect, you did as well. You sent me on a false assignment to prove what, that I was not the person I portray, to amuse yourself at my expense, or to watch my wither under pressure...

"Yes, you are correct," he said, cutting me off.

I was shocked.

"You're absolutely correct, but you forgot one, to teach you that your attitude is going to get you nowhere. So, I take no fault in this. It was all you and I don't call it being immature. I call it being your boss. I may have given you that assignment as a test, and I gave you help. Journey was your help, but you were too into yourself to realize it. That's when I realized what kind of person you are. Ms. Mills, you have a great natural talent for writing, but your ego counters it."

I was lost in my thoughts after what he said. I couldn't fault anyone but myself. Lequesha Johnson, my ego, my downfall, the leading lady cast in the role of my destruction, has used her power against me. I need to wipe her from my mind. I can't allow her to control my actions any longer.

I was knocked out of my trance when someone knocked on Mr. Kobe's door.

"Ms. Mills, if you are done, you may exit. Come in." he said to the person on the other side of the door.

The door opened to Journey walking in. We locked eyes for a moment before he preceded past me to Mr. Kobe.

"Journey, I apologize." I belted out making him stop in his tracks, "I apologize for everything," I repeated. "All you were trying to do was help and I acted immaturely and ungrateful."

Journey said nothing. He just looked at me with those piercing eyes. Mr. Kobe on the other hand was smiling.

"Ms. Mills, what has gotten into you. I have never seen this side of you before. Tell me, is this all an act or is this the new you?"

"Actually sir, this is the old me. The me before I was manipulated into becoming someone I was not." I responded back.

"Well this is a good look for you, and it is a pleasure to meet you."

Throughout the whole ordeal, Journey said nothing. He just continued with a poker face. I didn't know what to make of it, but my part was done. I felt better about myself because I was able to confront the two of them and apologize face to face.

As I glanced at the clock on Mr. Kobe's office wall, I remembered that Keith was in the car patiently waiting for me. I smiled at the two and left.

I walked out of the office relieved, this is the start of a new day. I stood outside a minute taking in the fresh Atlanta air; well, as fresh as it could be. Keith was in the car just smiling at me. I exhaled and started walking toward him.

"Tina, wait." I heard Journey say while hurrying to catch up to me.

"Thank you for apologizing. I do accept it. We are more alike than you may think. I also convinced Mr. Kobe to give you your job back. The article you wrote on the Williamsburg's assignment is what I used after I looked over it. They were able to piece it together and add it to what we had already written. It caught the eye of some big time people. So you are rehired. Please don't mess this up again. You really do have a talent for this."

"Thank you Journey I really appreciate that."

"I will call you to let you know the day you come back to work."

I was excited about getting my job back. Like I said, the start of my new day.

I got into the car and screamed with excitement. I'm too ecstatic about having my job back.

"This calls for a celebration. Tonight you, me, Yanza, and Corey are going out. Anywhere you want you want to go."

"Tonight, I want to go bowling."

"Then bowling it is." he said to me as he cracked the car up and drove off.

Chapter 8
Coffee House

I was in my room, back in my own bed relaxing and looking over my poetry book. I hadn't written in it in a long while.

"Hey Tina, I'm heading to the mall. I need some new heels for my show tonight. Did you want to come?" asked Yanza

"Yeah sure, I may see something that I may want to buy myself. Something sexy for me that Keith will enjoy."

"Oh girl, you so nasty," she said laughing, "But I'm ready whenever you are."

Within an hour we were cruising through Lenox Mall. I prefer Stonecrest or Cumberland because they are a little more in my price range, but at least I wouldn't be bored because there's always something going on at Lenox.

Yanza and I were doing more talking and acting a fool with each other more than shopping. The two of us really don't hang out together much outside of the apartment without the guys. So we were doing what ladies do when their boyfriends aren't around. We were checking out other men. It's nothing wrong with a little harmless flirting.

Yanza was doing most of the entertaining with other guys than I was. She was a natural. She had the guys wanting to buy us food, take us out, and some even wanted to buy clothes for us. She never accepted any of it because she said she is not a gold digger and didn't want to lead any of them on.

"The moment they buy you something, they think they own you." she said.

I laughed at the statement, but I agreed with it. One guy was persistent with trying to get her number. That wasn't going to happen. Corey would kill her. To get him off her back she asked for his number instead. She said she didn't have her phone with her so he could write it down. He did and with that we walked off. As soon as we were out of his sight, she tossed the paper in the trash.

"Girl he was too desperate. Even if I wasn't with Corey, I would never call him." she said.

"I know, he seemed to be one of those easily attached, overly possessive kinds."

"Oh My God!" Yanza said in shock, stopping in her tracks.

"Girl, what is it? What's wrong," I asked confused.

"You don't see those," she said walking into the store with me following behind still trying to figure out what she was talking about.

"My new babies. I have to have them in my life." she said

"Yanza seriously! All that over some shoes."

"Yes girl! You don't know heals like I know heals; double pump, open toe, zebra stripe finish. Dorathy ruby slippers has got nothing on these."

I just rolled my eyes and shook my head.

"Hello ladies, do you need any assistance," asked the sales attendant.

Yanza didn't hesitate to ask if he had these heels in a size 5.

"Wait here and I'll go check for you," he said.

While Yanza was waiting for her heels, I left to go to the lingerie store. It was only a few stores down from where the shoe store Yanza was in. This was my first time actually going lingerie shopping. The lady working the floor came over to assist me.

"Are you ok? Do you need a little help?" she asked me sweetly.

"Yes I do. I'm new to this so I don't know what I'm doing or looking for," I said.

"That's not a problem at all. May I ask if this is for a special occasion?"

"It is. Our anniversary is this weekend."

"Excellent! Well let me direct you to a section that is more suitable for you."

I didn't understand what she meant by more suitable, but I followed.

She led me to a section that was quite like the other one I was in, or so I thought until she started to explain the kind of lingerie I was looking at.

"Here we have a variety of lingerie suitable for special occasions such as anniversaries, birthdays, or for good behavior." she said pleasantly. "You have a nice frame, so maybe you would like a two piece to showcase it more, or if you want to be seductive and make him work for it, we have the one piece with garter belt or if he's anything like my husband and doesn't like to use any hands we have assort selection of edible arrangements." she said with a smile.

I was astonished, I never knew this kind of world existed; being raised by my brother and having to learn how to become a woman on my own, this was very surprising to me.

"How much are you looking to spend?" she asked.

"There is no price limit for this, He's worth it." I said.

"You got yourself a good one. Well honey do what you can to keep him happy if he is treating you right and keeping you happy as well. Now I will tell you what, I will walk you through this."

We spent the next two hours looking for something that both Keith and I would love. I brought them and left the store, realizing that I hadn't seen or heard from Yanza in a while, I walked back in the direction of the shoe store wondering if she was still there.

"Girl is that her right there, the one from the train," I heard someone say.

"Yes, that's her. I don't know what he sees in something like that. Looking like a two-dollar hooker from Cypress Street." I heard a girl say.

I continued to walk ignoring them because I knew good and well they weren't talking about me.

"So she gone act like she doesn't hear us?"

"Yeah because she knows what's good for her, and it ain't Keith, but he is all so right for me."

That there stopped me in my tracks. I turned around laughing at them. "You two are some sad individuals. What, you can't find your own man so you try to steal someone else's; and I did say try because Keith, my man Keith, don't want sluts like you."

"What did you just say," one of the girls asked.

"She best watch her tongue because this right here ain't what she want." the other girl said.

"You're right about that because none of that I want, but look here, I got what you want but you aren't going to get it." I shot back.

"Girl, I done had it and it was oh so good!"

"Yall are so funny to me, but you may have had a taste for one night, but listen here; I got it all the time." I responded back now realizing the crowd was picking up. Some of them already had their phones out to record, but I had put Laquesha Johnson to rest and I wasn't about to fight these tricks over something that is already mine.

"Do we have a problem here Tina that needs to be rectified," asked Yanza walking up from behind me.

"Girl no, these the tricks that were trying to get Keith." I told her.

"Okay, well let's go because we don't have time for the circus; so someone need to come get these monkeys and take them back to the zoo."

The crowd went up in an uproar. Everyone was dying at that comment.

"Who you calling a monkey," the girl said, taking off her earrings, feeling embarrassed.

"Girl put your fake bubble gum machine earrings back on. No one got time for you right now." said Yanza.

"Corey has all the time in the world for me," the other girl said.

"Girl, now you overstepping, but I'm just going to walk away because I can see how bad you want to become an overnight celebrity on World Star."

The girls started to walk up closer onto us.

"I am trying to be nice and save your lives but, you're asking for it. Tina I know you laid Lequesha

Johnson to rest but she needs to be resurrected right now."

With that said Yanza dropped her bags and connected with one of the girls. The girl's friend tried to jump in, but I grabbed her and in 1.2 seconds she was on the floor with punches to her face.

For a minute I heard nothing. I blacked out. I couldn't stop myself. I warned her. Yanza warned her. We even tried to walk away, but they kept coming. Since the day on the train they had it out for me. Then, when I went to Keith's house she started with me. Now here at the mall. It was the last straw.

Next thing I knew I was being pulled on by someone trying to get me off her. I wasn't going to go easy though because I wasn't finished. I wanted this girl to remember this so she wouldn't try to come after me again. I wanted her to fear my existence.

Whoever had me picked me up and was yelling for me to calm down. I was yelling back to let me go, to get off me. It was to no avail, he was strong and I couldn't break free.

I felt the rays of the sun and knew I was outside. I looked around and saw Corey holding Yanza back from attacking again. What was he doing here? I calmed down enough to see who had me and it was Keith. Where did they come from?

"If I put you down, you are not going to go attack them or me again," Keith asked.

"I'm fine. My point was made."

"Tina, are you okay," asked Yanza

"I'm great now."

"Good, let's go."

"Yanza, you are not driving anywhere upset." yelled Corey

"And who is going to stop me, you... I didn't think so."

"Why are you upset with me? What did I do?" Corey asked

"Can we take this elsewhere? I hear sirens." said Keith

"Yeah we should because Keith, you have some explaining to do." I said walking towards Yanza to get in her car.

I had nothing to say to him. He should've been handled this after I told him about how Tyneisha was acting towards me. He didn't so I did and now her friend put Corey and Yanza into it.

Chapter 9
Coffee House

Later that night it was still World War III in Yanza and my apartment. Corey confessed to keeping Tyneisha's friend company while Keith was with Tyneisha. He said they only talked. Every time she would come off too flirtatious, he would shut it down. Yanza's rebuttal was that he should've said something to her about it. He insisted he didn't tell her because it was a secret.

"It was a secret from Tina because of her surprise, not from me. If you had told me maybe all of this could've been avoided." she said walking into her room.

Keith on the other hand just looked defeated with the scratches on his face I gave him.

"Baby, please just talk to me," he begged.

"What is it you would like me to say Keith," I asked him

"I don't know, but something."

"Well Keith, I had said something; I have cried. I have been talked about behind my back and to my face, and now, Keith, because you didn't, I did something," I said coolly.

"Baby I'm sorry, but I was just trying to do something nice for you."

"By making a deal with the devil. But tell me something Keith, what was Tyneisha getting out of this? What is it you were giving up in return for her help," I asked him.

He went silent for a moment. He just looked at me. I was preparing myself for whatever he was going to tell me no matter how bad it was.

"I was tutoring her in statistics and we went out once with Corey and her friend to Burger World."

"A date," I yelled.

"No Tina, not a date."

"Keith was it all worth it? This surprise you have for me, that I still don't know about. Was it all worth it?"

"I didn't know it was going to turn out like this. You have to believe me," He said.

"I don't have to do anything, but you do. You need to leave," I commanded.

"Tina baby, I'm sorry. I messed up."

"Seems like that's something you do well." I said as I walked into my room while hearing Yanza kicking Corey out of her room and slamming the door.

I sat in my room just lost in my thoughts second guessing if I was too hard on Keith or not. Even though he went about it the wrong way he was still trying to do a good thing. Then the way he was apologizing and begging for my forgiveness with his sad puppy dog face was so cute. Maybe I was being too hard on him.

My phone rang and I saw it was Yanza. She asked me how I am doing? Seems like we both were thinking the same, maybe we were too hard on them. She told me how she can hear them talking with each other in the living area. She was saying how mad they are, not at us, but at those girls.

"Keith was really heated because he was like you and him are finally back at a good place and Tyneisha pulled a stunt like this," Yanza said.

"He's right, we are finally back in a good place. His heart was in the right place; maybe I should give him credit for that and forgive him," I said.

"Tina, this is how I look at it, I will forgive Corey, maybe I already have because their hearts were in the right place, but right now I'm about to teach him a little lesson so something like this won't happen again. About that Tyneisha girl and her friend, I fought her because she disrespected me not over Corey because I don't have to fight over something that is already mine. You need to figure out for yourself how to handle this situation. It's clear as day that Keith loves you, or else he would not be out there right now trying to work on a way for you to forgive him. It's obvious Tyneisha thought she had a chance with Keith so her job was to break you two up so she can move in. Don't give her the satisfaction."

"You are right girl, and I hope this surprise that I still know nothing about is worth all of this."

"Guess you will have to wait and see." Yanza said, smiling through the phone.

"That's right he did tell you when I was in the hospital."

"Yes he did, and I was sworn to secrecy, so you'll have to wait. But I forgot to tell you the hospital called. They were trying to contact you, but they couldn't reach you. They want you to call them. They said it's important."

"It wasn't that important if you forgot to tell me about it," I said laughing.

"HAHA funny, but girl come out here, let's have a movie night with the guys. I'm cooled down now and could use some TLC."

"Okay, I'm coming after I take this call from Journey."

"Let me know when you're ready so we can make our dramatic entrance. They need to grovel some more."

"Yanza you are crazy."

"I'm not crazy but I am a teacher and the lesson has just begun."

"And Keith will learn too, but let me answer this call."

I felt a lot better after talking with Yanza. She put into perspective the kind of boyfriend I have. I already knew Keith was special, but now I see it's deeper than just that.

I clicked over to answer Journey's call. To my surprise he presented me with an opportunity I never expected to have. He told me how much The Board loved my article. They want to tell my story for an article they are working about personality disorder. I told him I will think about it and get back with him. I asked when I should report back to work, he said to enjoy my weekend and to be in the office on Monday morning.

"I will Journey and thank you for everything." I said to him.

"You're welcome." he responded before hanging the phone up.

I was excited about having my job back. It seemed like everything was starting to fall into place for me. I screamed a silent scream to not alarm anyone, then texted Yanza to let her know I was headed to the living room. I put on my poker face because Keith is going to learn this lesson.

I walked out into the living area to see both Corey and Keith seating on the sofa with blankets. Keith and I made eye contact and his face lit up. He motioned with his hand to the blanket as if to invite me in to cuddle with him. I heard the microwave sound and looked up to see Yanza fixing popcorn. We made eye contact, and spoke with them saying the lesson was on. I walked over to Keith and sat beside him as he wrapped the blanket around the two of us.

Yanza approached with the popcorn and Corey did the same to her. These guys didn't know what was coming their way, but they were about to find out. Corey started the movie and the rest of the night was peaceful.

Chapter 10
Coffee House

Over the next few days, Keith and Corey had been the perfect gentlements. They would do anything Yanza and I asked of them. And I do mean anything. Keith for sure learned to not put me back in this kind of situation again.

"Bae, am I out of the dog house yet," Keith asked, trying to sound innocent.

I walked up to him to give him a kiss. He smiled and pulled me into a hug and said he loves me. I repeated I loved him as I was leaving for the office.

"Tina, the question, am I still in the doghouse?"

"I love you Keith." I said smiling because it was cute to know how much he loves me. Tomorrow night was our anniversary and that was when Keith would be off of punishment.

This was my second day back at work. Yesterday was a trying one because everyone was gossiping trying to figure out how I got my job back. One girl even started the rumor about me sleeping with Mr. Kobe because he was known for his ruthless attitude, and that would have been the only way I could've softened him up enough to give me my job back. I ignored it all and went about my day, but I couldn't help but notice one girl, the one that started the rumor, was mean mugging me all day. Journey said it was all in my head and to just focus on the assignment that we had.

Journey was also asked to write his own views into the personality disorder assignment. He further explained that a few others were also selected to add their views into the article as well. He didn't want to do it at first, but after some convincing he finally agreed to it, but only because I was willing to.

Journey once told me he had a past, but I shook it off because no one's past couldn't have been worse than mine. I was about to find out how wrong I was.

I was ready for the day. I was going to show Mr. Kobe the new me. I was ready for my story to be out so everyone could understand the old me. Even though that same girl was eyeballing me, I ignored her. I don't know what her deal was, but La'Tina Mills, yes that's right, La'Tina Mills, didn't have time for it.

I made my way to my desk to put my things away and before I could sit down Journey called me into his office. He looked a little hysterical and seemed like he was about to suffer a panic attack, so I rushed in to ask what was wrong.

"I can't do it Tina," He said breathlessly.

"Calm down Journey... breath."

"I'm breathing, that I can do. Writing the story, I can't do." he said, sitting in his chair holding his head down. "It's too painful to relive, so I'd chosen to forget and that was the best thing that happened to me. I became the man I was meant to be. Maybe a great man."

"Journey you saw my story, it wasn't all glitz and glamour."

"I know Tina, and I'm not trying to compare our past, but I would've given anything to have a piece of that life you had." he said.

I was speechless, for him to say he would take my past over his. He must have had a hellish one. I went to give him a hug to let him know he doesn't have to tell his story.

"Journey, I need the format to the..., oh! I see Mr. Kobe wasn't enough." the same girl that was mean mugging me said as she entered Journey's office.

"3, 2, 1, 1, 2, 3, breath," I said to myself.

"Anything for you to get ahead," she continued

"Girl, who are you?" Better yet it's not important," I shot back at her.

"Felicia, what are you here for?" Journey asked

"I came here for the format to the Harrison and McClaine features of the article."

"The format has been changed and Mr. Kobe has the new one, you can receive it from him," Journey instructed.

Felicia just stood there looking at me with evil eyes. If looks could kill, I would be lower than 6ft.

"Is that all Felicia," asked Journey

She said nothing but still gave me that death stare before leaving and heading out of the office.

"Now do you believe me about her," I asked Journey.

"Calm down Tina, but yes I do. Do you two know one another from somewhere?"

"Not outside of these walls. Barely inside for that matter."

"I will take care of it, and I commend you on how you handled yourself," he said smiling

"I just got my job back and I'm not trying to lose it, but don't let that fool you."

Journey just smiled at me with those pearly white teeth. My knees began to give out a little. He caught me and sat me in his chair asking me if I was all right. I nodded yes.

"Are you sure you're okay, because this isn't the first time I've seen this happen to you," Journey asked again.

"How is everything going in here," asked Mr. Kobe, sticking his head into Journey's office.

"Everything is going great." Journey and I replied in unison.

"That's what I like to hear. How are the stories coming along?"

"Well, we ran into a little roadblock-"

"That we've worked our way through, all we need is one day extension." I said cutting Journey off.

Mr. Kobe looked lost at first like he didn't know what to believe but he granted the extension and left the office.

Journey looked at me because he had already stated he wasn't about to dig into his past. I told him I understood his pain and that he didn't have to write about it. I told him my idea of combining both of our pasts and create a new person. I explain to him that this way no one will know his struggles and we can still pull off the article for Mr. Kobe. He was still a bit unsettled with the idea, but he preferred this opposed to using his actual identity.

We worked hard for the remainder of the day on the story. We learned a lot about one another and now I see why he said he would trade my past for his. I don't think I would've been able to survive.

By the end of the day my eyes were dry from all the tears I'd shed. Journey even shed a few as well. We were bonded for life because he said this was the first time he'd opened up to anyone about his past. He also said he felt a little better about it. I told him he could open up to me more so he could be free from his it. He responded with a simple head nod and a smile.

I looked at the time to see it was going on 6pm. I never enjoyed the short days and longer night season because it always made it seem later than what it was.

Walking out of the building, the last person I wanted to see was the first person I saw still giving me that death stare. I ignored it again and continued on my way out to catch my train. As I was walking, I started to hear footsteps coming up from behind me, she was following me. Once we reached outside she started a verbal attack on me. I still didn't pay her any attention because I still didn't know who the girl was or what her issue was with me and I really didn't care to know.

"Oh, so you are weak without your little sidekick," she touted.

I stopped for a brief second then continued to walk. I just don't know why people are always testing me. Lequeisha Johnson was put to rest but they wouldn't let her stay there.

"You think that little show you put on at the mall was something, well I'm the true fighter in the family." she said advancing towards me

I stopped because now I got it.

"The tricks at the mall was your family? So you want the same treatment they got," I asked

"This time it will be you being sent to the hospital." she said, preparing to attack.

"Do we have a problem here ladies," asked Mr. Kobe walking up on us. "Felicia, do we?" he said again more strunned.

"We don't," she replied

"Ms. Mills, do we," he asked, directing his attention to me.

"No sir," I said.

"Good, so why don't you be on your way. Felicia, I want to have a word with you."

"This isn't over, Tina," Felicia threatened

"Oh but it is and I will make sure that it is. You see Felicia when you start rumors about me, make sure your facts are more accurate. So let's go have a chat in my office and if I hear about you coming after Ms. Mills again here or elsewhere. You will have way more to deal with besides what we are about to go and discuss. Do I make myself clear young lady?"

"Yes father." she responded.

"Now go, and you have a good night Ms. Mills," he said smiling at me.

I was speechless. The look on my face at this moment was priceless. I didn't know she was his daughter, and she had the nerve to start a rumor about him. If only I could be a fly on his office wall for that conversation. I was just having a gay old time as I continued my walk to the transit station. This day could not have ended any better.

Chapter 11
Coffee House

I feel the light, It calls out to me
Welcoming, warm embrace
Naturing sounds that soothes my soul
I want to go to it, enter into it

But I am trapped
Being held down by an entity
A powerful force that pulls me into the dark
It wants me, It accepts me, It appreciates me
And yet I fear it.
I don't know what will become of me,
My soul to be a lost treasure
My exist to vanish
No echo in the wind
Not even a footprint left in the sand
But the light,
It heals me, It believes in me, It longs for me
The fight within me masked by my outer shell
A dwelling tug of war that no other eye can see
I have became the rope of desire
Being pulled, hoping the rightful ruler be the
victor
The light to suppress the dark
The dark to cover the light

Thinking back over my life as I read over some of the poems I'd written, my life had been a war with me being tugged in every direction. I smiled and laughed at it because of where I was in my life. My poetry book had become a sort of diary to look back and see what I had been through and to see how much my writing had improved.

After I got settled in last night I called Journey to see if he was okay after the emotional day we'd had, and to tell him what happened. He didn't know Felicia was Mr. Kobe's daughter either. He was shocked, but also seemed a bit upset by it. I asked why but he said it was nothing. I think I know what it is. I'd been putting the pieces together, but when he told me his story it confirmed it for me. I didn't care about it, he was my friend no matter what and when he was ready to confess to me I would be there to listen.

I got up from the bed and walked over to the window pulling the curtains back to welcome the morning. Today was the day of mine and Keith's anniversary. I had been planning it for a while. I had the new lingerie and I knew Keith had never seen me in anything like that. I was planning on pulling out everything. Keith wanted nothing more but to apologize and make things right between us, tonight he would bear the fruit of his labor.

Later that morning, before Keith left out with Corey, I picked a little argument with him. I knew I was playing with fire, but I told Corey and Yanza my plan so they would calm him down until I put my thing on him tonight. He was confused because it came out of nowhere. I was laughing so hard in my head at that moment because he was so cute. Corey was laughing as well behind Keith's back as he tried to get him out the door.

Everything was going perfectly. Yanza came over to the guy's place to help me set up. Keith had always talked about going to Hawaii, unfortunately, I couldn't afford a trip there so turning his house into a Hawaiian resort was the next best thing. Now, all I needed was my Hawaiian shirt, my coconut bra, and coconut cups delivered. I had a Hawaiian feast catered, and I had learned some Hawaiian dances to have a mini Luau. I was going to blow his mind because he'd never expect me to do something to that magnitude, but Keith was worth every penny.

Corey told me everything Keith had planned for me except the big secret he had used Tyneisha's help for. I spoke to the managers of the restaurant and the hotel he was taking me to, I was able to cancel everything and get his deposit. Of course they wouldn't give it to me, so I asked if they could hold all information about it until after our anniversary so Keith wouldn't expect a thing.

Pretending to have been Keith's wife had me thinking I much I couldn't wait to become Mrs. Keith Williams for real. He was my first love and I wanted him to become my last. I knew we were still young, so rushing into marriage was something I wouldn't do. Slow and steady win the race and baby this was one race I intend to win.

Yanza and I were close to finishing the decorations but I still hadn't received my delivery yet.

"Girl, this place is looking amazing. I'm a little jealous right now," said Yanza

"I know, I'm impressed myself, but Keith will be here soon and my delivery still hasn't arrived yet."

"When did they say it would be here," Yanza asked.

I went over to get my phone to look up the itinerary. It told me it was supposed to be here sometime between 12pm-5pm.

"Tina, you need to call them because it's almost 8 o'clock," said Yanza

Looking at the time, she was right. I was so busy decorating that I didn't realize the time. I dialed the number that was on the itinerary, there was no answer.

"What am I going to do? Everything needs to be perfect. I need the coconut bra and the shirt."

"Can you improvise with something else?"

I gave her a dark look because she knew good and well I didn't have anything like that.

"I hate to be the bearer of more bad news Tina, but Corey just texted me, he and Keith will be pulling up shortly."

"NO NO NO" I shouted, "Can't he ride him around the neighborhood some more?"

"Too late, they're here."

I ran to the window and peaked out. Corey was pulling into the driveway, along with my delivery, which had finally arrived.

I had to get out there before Keith started questioning the driver. Yanza said she would stall Keith for as long as she could so I can get the remaining things set up. She's truly my girl, my ride or die. I'm lucky to have someone like her in my life.

As we were walking outside, I kept up my charade like I was still upset with Keith.

"What are you doing here," I snarled as I walked past him.

"I live here...I can't believe she is still upset, and for what I still don't know," he said to Corey.

I continued my walk to the delivery driver. He saw the face I was wearing and quickly started in on his delivery resolution.

"Are you La"Tina Mills," he asked ,and I just nodded my head yes, "I apologize for being late, my truck broke down. Can you sign right here please?" he said as he pointed to where I needed to sign.

I did as I was told. The driver apologized again before returning to his truck and driving off. The entire time Keith was looking at what was going on.

"What is that Tina...girl talk to me," he pleaded.

I still said nothing, I just walked in the house while Yanza started working her magic.

After I got into the house and closed the door I kicked into overdrive. I was breaking in the packages like a kid on Christmas morning. I only had a few seconds to kick my clothes off and into the Hawaiian outfit. I had to do a superman phone booth change.

When I was done. I turned off all the lights in the house and waited for my man to walk through the doors. I can hear them conversing outside trying to convince Keith to come in.

"Why should I, she treated me like a dog the whole day and I still don't know what I did," I heard him say.

"So go find out," said Yanza

"Yea mayne, just go in there and talk to her," Corey chimed in.

"Yall females are crazy, I swear. She better be glad I love her to the moon and back."

I heard him walking up the stairs. I was excited to see his reaction. Everything took a lot of planning, and I prayed that everything went right and the moment was finally here.

Keith slowly opened the door and peeked in, he noticed all the lights were off and didn't want to enter.

"Why is it so dark in here," he yelled out to Yanza and Corey

"Mayne, man up and go face your woman." Corey yelled back

"Okay, but if y'all don't hear from me tomorrow, let my parents and Kyle know I love them very much."

I was trying hard not to laugh at his dramatic self.

"Baby...Tina." he called out as he was turning on the lights

"Welcome to Hawaii, where all your dreams will come true." I said causing his spirit to jump out of him.

After he regained himself, he was in awe at how the place looked. The only thing missing was the volcano.

"Is this your first time visiting the islands of Hawaii," I asked as I placed the garland around his neck. He stuttered out a yes.

"You are speechless? The Hawaii Islands are a breathtaking place. Great memories of life changing events happens here."

"Tina, I can't believe you did all this for me." he said in shock

"I am sorry sir, but you have me confused. My name is Akela, but it's said that everyone has a twin somewhere in the world," he looked at me and just grinned.

"You have arrived on a special day of celebrating. It is a special annual event. I will be your tour guide throughout your stay here. How were your travels here?" I said

"It was okay, I'm just glad to have finally arrived," Keith responded, starting to play along.

"Come with me to one of our paradise beaches where there are feasts fit for a king, along with a special Luau tonight," with that I led Keith to where I had created a beach with beach chairs, sand, and a pool filled with crystal water.

"Now sit right here and just admire the ocean."

I sat him down while the breeze blew through the Hawaiian trees and the sound of the ocean played through a projector that played on the wall. The way Keith's face lit up made me feel special. He deserved this.

"What are you doing?" I asked slightly shocked.

"I wanted my feet in the sand," he said.

"I will take care of that for you," I said back to him as I began to take off his shoes and socks to place them in the sand, "How does that feel?"

"I am in heaven right now."

"This is good. I will go and prepare The Feast."

I started to walk away from Keith. My heart was smiling because he was enjoying himself. He couldn't stop smiling from ear to ear.

"What are you doing," I asked walking back towards him

"I was a thirty, I was going to get some of that punch."

"You insult Akela," I said rushing over to get some punch, "You're trying to get me fired by doing things on your own."

"I'm sorry, I didn't know that was policy," he said.

"Well now you do so don't let it happen again," I said smiling as I was returning to ready his Feast.

"I just wanted to say, Akela, you are wearing that skirt."

"Why thank you. I'm glad you approve," I replied back.

I was watching Keith admiring his Hawaiian resort. This was the closest he had gotten to Hawaii. One day I will take him there but for now our Imagination will run wild tonight.

"Akela, what is on the menu tonight?"

"Are you ready to eat? Tonight we have Hawaiian Roasted Kalua Pork that was prepared traditionally. It gives it a taste mainlanders can't compare, with chicken long rice, and Aloha Sweet Potatoes. Then, for dessert, we are serving Pineapple Butterscotch Squares and Macadamia Coconut Cake."

"All that sounds great Akela," Keith said.

"Well it will taste even better." I said walking over to him with his food.

Keith was just staring at me. He seemed mesmerized by my appearance. If he thinks this outfit is something, just wait until he saw what I brought from the mall, I thought to myself.

I handed him his food.

"May I replace your punch with a Mai Tai or a Blue Hawaiian Cocktail perhaps," I asked.

"You have real Mai Tais," he asked excitedly.

"And why would it not be real? You forget, you are in the islands of Hawaii."

"I've always wanted to try it."

"Then tonight is the night," I said to him as I went to get his Mai Tai.

I started to play the music for my Luau dance. Suddenly, the alarm sounded and Keith started to look around alarmed, wondering what was happening. I hurried back to him with his Mai Tai.

"It is time." I shouted

"Time for what?"

"Showtime."

It was the start of the Luau. I ran to the beach area where I had set up more sand near where the projector was located. The alarm stopped and the music began, and so did my hips. This dance took me months to master, and I have been practicing on and off throughout that time.

Keith was entranced with the way I was swaying my hips. It was like he was the snake and I was charming him with my body instead of a flute. I just wanted to give him an authentic Hawaiian experience, and I think I was achieving that.

When the song ended Keith was standing, applauding, and whistling, but it wasn't over yet. Out of nowhere, drums started and the music began again, more of an uptempo beat. I began dancing, this time I stepped off my plateau and went to him, dancing around him. At one point he stood and began to dance along with me. He was having such a good time.

Finally, I went back to go back to the beach area to finish my routine. I grabbed ribbons to add a bit more excitement to the ending. I was blowing his mind. He couldn't believe I went to such levels for him. His eyes were telling me everything his mind was thinking.

I ended the show with an array of glitter tossed into the air, the reflection off the projector making it look as if stars were shining in the night. Seeing that was breathtaking. I was amazed at how everything turned out.

"Akela, this has been the best night, anniversary, and relationship I've ever had. Can you do something for me," he asked.

"Sure, I am here for you."

"When you see Tina, can you tell her that I really appreciate all of this, that I really appreciate her, and that I love her with my heart. Tell her that the words have yet to be invented to express what I'm feeling right now. She's the greatest. She is truly and ultimately my soul mate. Also, Akela, could you tell Tina one more thing for me?"

Before I could say yes, he kissed me and tears fell down my cheek.

That kiss opened up heaven for me. God looked down and smiled because this creation he had brought together amazed him. That kiss made me feel more alive than I'd ever felt. With that kiss he became my Adam and I his Eve.

He broke away from me and stared into my eyes.

"I love you La'Tina Mills."

"I love you too, and Happy Anniversary."

Keith held me and I was at a state of peace and I became lost in his arms.

Chapter 12
Coffee House

The next day, I was on cloud nine at work. Volcanoes erupted last night, but not in the way I thought they were going to. Keith didn't hold anything back. His focus was completely on me, neglecting all of his needs, and I was ready to get back to that.

I came in on my day off, to what was supposed to had been a half day of work, to help Journey with changes to the Personality Disorder assignment the editor insisted we make, ended up being longer because Journey had been dragging from the negative mood he was in. I didn't press the issue on why, figuring he would come out and tell me himself. Whatever it was, it was eating at him and starting to worry me. In the time I'd known him, I'd never seen him like this. He was the spunky one.

"Hey Journey, we're about done here, can you give me a ride to Keith's house," I asked.

Sure, was all he said.

I waited outside Journey's office as he shut down his computer. He was moving like a snail and I wasn't used to this. I didn't know how to act around this person in front of me right now.

As we were walking out of the building the last person I wanted to see caught my eyes. She glared at me before continuing to do whatever it was she was doing. I guess her little talk with daddy did her some justice.

We got to Journey's car and got in with him still in that zombie state. I was too excited about mine and Keith's date that night. I would finally know this big secret. I just couldn't show my excitement because of how Journey felt. I would like to share my excitement with him, but I didn't think it would make whatever he's dealing with better.

"Journey, look out," I yelled out to keep him from running through the traffic light and causing a collision.

"I'm so sorry Tina," he said breathlessly, "are you okay?"

"I'm fine, but it's clear you're not, so you need to pull the car over. You are transporting precious cargo and you need to handle it with care."

"Tina, I can drive you to your boyfriend's house, you don't have to get out." he said, pulling the car over to the side of the street.

"I wasn't going to get out, we're going to sit here and talk about this mood you've been in today. It doesn't look good on you and I'm not used to seeing you like this."

"So you're going to force me to talk," he said defeatedly.

"Yes, because it's affecting you. Look at what just happened, you almost ran through a red light. Besides, I'm your friend, you can tell me anything. You should know that by now." I said trying to console him.

"I know Tina, but it's not my secret alone to tell."

When he said that, in the moment, I knew what it was. I looked at him for a minute before giving him a hug. I gracefully whispered in his ear that I knew. He looked at me with confusion as I released him while I repeated to him again that I knew, and he didn't have to say anything.

"You never said anything," he said

"It was nothing that needed to be said. It doesn't change anything. But now what you need to do is talk it out and you know with whom I am speaking of."

"I will once the dust is settled, I guess, but how did you figure all this out?"

"I paid attention."

He smiled that beautiful smile of his.

"Now that looks good on you."

"Thank you, Tina. Now let me get you to Keith before he has my head for keeping you."

After pulling up to Keith's house, Keith was waiting for me on the porch. I was excited that I practically jumped out of the car before it came to a complete stop which made Journey laugh. I was finally about to find out what my big surprise was.

"I'm sorry for being late, work took longer than I thought it was going to," I said to Keith, meeting him at the door.

"It's okay bae, but go get cleaned up while I speak with Journey for a minute."

I was taken back by that statement but I shook it off and ran into the house coming out of my clothes with every step I took.

I took a quick shower to wash away the day. The water was soothing against my skin. My mind was free until I started wondering what Keith needed to speak to Journey about, but again, I shook it off. Minutes later I was out of the shower and in the bedroom pulling a dress out of my side of the closet. This is new for me because I hadn't never worn a dress or the type of lingerie I bought from the mall. This is definitely going to be a night to remember on many levels.

The long evening gown with a slit that revealed my right thigh made me a bit uncomfortable. As I looked at myself in the mirror, I was amazed at how I looked. I felt like a princess, something I never thought I would feel. Yanza walked into the room as I was still admiring myself, she was in awe with me as I was with her. She was curvaceous and the gown she wore hid nothing to the imagination.

"You look amazing Tina," she said.

"Thank you, but what are you doing here."

"This is a part of your surprise; are you about ready?"

"I am, but I don't know if I can do these heels girl. They are already hurting my feet."

"This is why you take house shoes as well. Once we get there you can change into them."

"We?"

"Surprise, now come on the guys are waiting," she said while laughing.

"What are you all up too," I asked

"You will just have to wait and see. Also, did you call your doctor yet because he called again."

"I haven't but I will tomorrow."

"Make sure you do. He sounded like it was urgent that you did."

"I promise I will tomorrow. Now come on, my surprise is awaiting me."

We stepped out to present ourselves to the guys. From the look on his face, I think I took Keith's breath away.

"Tina is that you, I mean, wow," he said

"I'm glad you like it," I said shyly.

"I love it."

Corey made a facial suggestion to get Keith to regain his composure. Keith did as he fixed his tie and jacket on his three piece European cut suit.

"La'Tina Mills, tonight is a special night. Tonight, the King and Queen of the Sundial Tower Gala are requesting your presence and I was charged to oversee your safe arrival. Do you accept the invitation?"

"Yes I dot." I relied blushing

"Excellent! Right this way. Your chariot awaits."

When Keith opened the door I saw that the way was covered in a red carpet with white lights leading to a white and gold chariot pulled by two white horses.

"Keith," was all I could get out of the mouth. I couldn't find the words to express my amazement.

"Right this way," he said, holding out his hand for me.

I grabbed it and he led me to the chariot followed by Corey and Yanza. The coachman waited patiently with the door open for us to enter.

"This is something straight out of a fairy tale." I uttered breathlessly.

"You are my Cinderella as long you don't run off and leave me at midnight."

"I will never leave you Keith," I said as he placed a kiss on his lips.

I'd ridden through the streets of Atlanta by bus, by train, and by car, but that night the city lights were more magical. I was speechless at the sight. It was unbelievable.

"How do you like it," Keith asked

"I love it Keith," I responded with Corey and Yanza both saying "AWW" in unison.

"You are saying aww now, Corey but you know Yanza is going to expect nothing less than this for you all's anniversary," I said to him laughing. Corey just laughed until Yanza gave him a look.

"She is right. I hope you know."

"Bae," Corey responded with his sad puppy dog face.

We all burst out laughing.

"We are about there Mr. Williams," the coachman said.

"This night is just beginning," Keith said as we made the final approach to the Sun Dial.

I had always passed this Sun Dial but I'd never been inside it. The ride to the top was unbearable for me with my fear of heights. But tonight, I was with my prince so I would conquer that fear.

We stepped out of the chariot. The breeze made the air a little chilled but still nice out for fall weather. We walked inside to locate the elevator. The SunDial was at the top of the towel, about 40 floors up. We perceived into the glass elevator with others going up as well. The view from the elevator overseeing the city as it rose was exquisite, I'd never seen the city from that point of view before.

"How do you feel," Keith asked me.

"No words can describe this feeling."

"You took me to Hawaii so allow me to take you to heaven," he said as the door of the elevator opened.

"Oh my god! Keith, how did you?"

"This is your night bae, so nothing is being held back. I've been planning this for a while with the help of Corey and a few others."

I looked over at Yanza to see she was feeling the same way I was glad to have had the experience with her as well.

"I love you Keith." I said looking into his eyes.
"I love you too."

He led me to where we were to be seated. The room was filled with luxurious things from the crystal dolphins to real angels hanging from the ceiling. This was the ball I'd dreamt about as a child. I never would have believed it would come true.

"Tina, there's one thing I have to do. I'll be right back," Keith said as he grabbed Corey and vanished into the crowd.

"Girl, did you know about this," I asked Yanza.
"I didn't know about all of this. They left me out of the loop too," she said.

We talked some more about the night as we continued to wait for Keith and Corey. I noticed the one person I didn't want to see, I didn't know why, but Tyneisha was not going to ruin this night for me. I also laid eyes on two other persons I didn't expect to be here, we made eye contact and they began to walk towards Yanza and I.

"My Tina, I must admit you are wearing that dress," said Journey.

"Yes Ms. Mills, you clean up quite nicely," added Mr. Kobe

"Thank you to both of you, but what are you doing here? I didn't expect to see you here tonight."

"Keith invited me, he told me I had to come and the boss man here wasn't doing anything tonight. I didn't want to come alone, so here we are," said Journey

"Well I'm glad you both are here. Mr. Kobe, I would like you to meet my best friend Yanza. Yanza this is my boss, Mr. Kobe."

"Pleasure to meet you. I remember you from the article Ms. Mills wrote about you. It was a very interesting piece," said Mr. Kobe

Yanza smiled and said thank you.

A few hours into the ball and my feet were starting to hurt. Keith was kind enough to massage them for me and it felt good. Everyone was enjoying themselves. Keith disappeared into the crowd again and moments later I heard his voice.

I was looking around for him but still couldn't see him. He was singing over the microphone. He has a beautiful voice but he never shows it.

Finally I saw him walking towards me through a fog of smoke. It was like he was gliding towards me.

'How and Now. I promise to love faithfully. You're all I need. Here and Now. I vow to be one with thee. Your love is all I need.'

Keith grabbed my hand and pulled me towards him.

"Tina, you are my life. My day starts and ends with the thoughts of you. You stood with me through my dark years and when my family had to leave without a trace, you never forgot me. You are my angel. You guide me in the right direction. You are my world and without you there is no me."

Keith was saying all these things and the tears were just falling. He started to get down on one knee and my heart started pounding.

"La'Tina Mills, will you do me the greatest honor in becoming my wife."

I was holding my chest. This is what I've been wanting. This is what I've been waiting for.

"Tina!" Keith said

My heart was still pounding. I looked into Keith's hazel eyes.

"Yes Keith, I will."

The whole room went up in a roar of applause. Even Tyneisha was applauding.

'Starting here, ooh I'm starting right now. I believe in love. I'm starting here, I'm starting right here. Right now because, I believe in your love so I'm glad to take a vow here and now.'

Keith kissed me like he had never kissed me before. This is truly my Cinderella story, I had my prince.

"Tina I can admit now that Tynesha was one of the main people helping me plan all this. She made this night affordable because of her position in the city. I couldn't tell you all that without ruining your surprise." he tells me.

Now it all made sense. She saw what Keith was planning for me. She saw that he was a good man and she wanted him for herself. I'm glad the love for me is deeper than physical. I'm glad he loved me with his whole heart.

"Excuse me one moment."I said as I was beginning to do the unthinkable. I was walking over to Tyneisha to thank her for everything she had done for Keith and I. She said I was welcome and complimented me on my dress and said congratulations. I thanked her again and walked off back towards the others but met Yanza before getting to everyone.

"Congratulations girl. You deserve this. You two was always great together. I saw you and Tyneisha, that was big of you."

"Thank you Yanza. Keith told me how she helped him with this night so I simply went over to thank her," I said with a smile.

"Girl that's right," Yanza said as we high five.

"You are my girl for life," I said, making us both laugh.

The rest of the night was a blur. Women started taking their heels off and the guys were coming out of their coats. It was a night to remember.

It was getting late and close to closing time; instead of the horse drawn chariot, Keith ordered a car. Keith and I went back to his house to turn down for the night, while Corey and Yanza continued on to her apartment. Keith doesn't know but I have one more surprise for him.

I told Keith to get comfortable while I go freshened up.

"The future Mrs. Keith Williams come on out that bathroom, I'm lonely out here," Keith called out.

I was struggling to get the dress off. It was easy to get on but much harder to get off.

"I'm coming." I called back.

I finally was able to free myself of the dress. Before heading to the room I freshened up, making sure to adjust my lingerie and to put on the Red Bottoms Heels that Yanza let me borrow for the night. Looking in the mirror, I saw that I was ready. Let's go I thought as I headed to give Keith the time of his life.

"Here I am my future husband to be." I said while posing in the bedroom doorway.

Keith did a double take. "Are you serious right now? Bring all that sexy over here," he said while motioning me closer.

"Do you think you can handle all this sexy." I asked while slowly walking towards him.

"Come here and let me show you," he said before pulling me closer to him and looking me in the eyes, "I love you La' Tina Mills."

"I love you too Keith." I said as I allowed him to lay me down before giving myself over to him.

Chapter 13
Coffee House

I woke up in a strange place that felt as if I had been there before, unafraid because it was warm and peaceful. I called out to Keith, but there was no answer. "How did I end up here," I wondered. Last I remembered was the night before, was it all a dream? It couldn't have been, this place here, this place I was in right now was the dream. I called out Keith's name again, but still no answer. Last night was so magical, so it had to have been real. Keith proposed to me. It was a dream came true, and the ring he gave me was so beautiful. I was really Cinderella at the ball last night.

My ring, where was my ring? No, it couldn't have been a dream. Keith where are you? I questioned again but still no answer. I was beginning to get worried.

"Tina," a voice called out.

I looked, but did not see anyone.

"Tina, you're safe here," said the voice. Somehow it sounded familiar.

"Daddy?"

"Tina," the voice said again.

I looked and saw something coming toward me. I was nervous because I didn't know what it could be.

"Baby Girl," the voice said

"How is this possible? This has to be a dream." I said now convinced it was.

"It's okay baby girl. This is sort of like a dream." he said.

"I've missed you so much," I said hugging him tightly.

"I have missed you too. I've always been here watching over you. I'm so proud of the woman you've become."

All I could do was cry. My father, I was actually hugging my father again and I could feel him holding me as well. I'd missed that touch. I've always felt safe in his arms.

"Everything is going to be okay now Tina."

"I know daddy, my life right now is perfect. I'm engaged. If only you were here to walk me down the aisle."

"That's wonderful. I always knew you would be okay despite your brother's influences on you.

You've made me a proud father...but right now Tina you need to come with me. I need to explain something to you."

I began to back away from him slowly and looked in his eyes. Thoughts of my grandmother's wisdom started to echo in my head. She would tell me if I ever dreamt about the dead, I may speak to them, but I should never follow them because they would lead you to your death. I love my father and I miss him every day, but dying at that point in my life wasn't on my agenda.

"Daddy, I love you, but I cannot follow you."

"But you must, I have a lot to explain to you," he said while holding out his hand for me to grab.

I ran from him. I ran to wake myself up. I don't want to die. I started yelling Keith's name hoping he would hear me and wake me up.

I froze in my tracks when I finally heard his voice, but it wasn't just his voice I heard, I heard Yanza's and Corey's as well. What was going on? I could hear them as if I were right there with them. They sound sad.

"Tina, please don't leave me. You said you would never leave me." Keith sobbed out

"I'm right here, I'm not going anywhere! Why can't I wake up? I want to wake up."

An unfamiliar voice began to speak, saying that it was time. It had been months with no change. If they had caught it in time things would have been different.

"This can't be happening," I heard Keith say.

"Keith come here," I heard Yanza say.

"No, it's not fair! She's my soulmate! It's just not fair," Keith cried out

"We will get through this mayne," I heard Corey say.

"NO!"

"GO AFTER HIM." shouted Yanza, crying herself

"I truly am sorry." the other voice said.

"No this can't be." I said falling to my knees. My life was going so right. I don't want to die.

"I will help you through it Baby Girl," my father said as he placed his hand on my shoulder, "Come with me."

I looked up at him still not wanting to believe. The moment I received my happiness, it was taken away from me in a blink of an eye. Poetic Justice.

Bear the image I portray
Against the me I am inside

The wrath became me
So I can't deny the fate

But the fate I have to bear

Because of her that is not I

Illuminates the illusion within
That my innocents is justified

I am who I was, the first
The rest, I can no longer identify

So should I be damned to her fate
Or should I be willed to escape

A paradise, invisions of life to maintain
Hiding the lure of a shy insecure dame

If respectfully embracing the trust so dark
That without her, it was no me

Bringing our destinies to intertwine
Uncanny to think my happiness a lie

And I am the evil within the light
Revealed in the mirror the truth

That she is me and me is I

Special thanks to Pearl W. for the artwork

Contact Information for Kiroh:

www.Kiroh-The-Author.com
Instagram @ Kirohtheauthor58
Twitter @ kirohtheauthor

Made in the USA
Middletown, DE
03 August 2023